FROM THE
EDGE
OF THE
CROWD

FROM THE EDGE OF THE CROWD

OF THE

CROWD

Meditations for Lent

JAMES E. SARGENT

UPPER ROOM BOOKS®
NASHVILLE

FROM THE EDGE OF THE CROWD
Meditations for Lent
© 2003 by James E. Sargent
All rights reserved.

The Upper Room® Web site: www.upperroom.org.

Cover and interior design: Gore Studio Inc.
Cover image: Getty Images
First printing: 2003

LIBRARY OF CONGRESS CATALOGING-IN-PUBLICATION DATA
Sargent, James E.
    From the edge of the crowd : meditations for Lent / James E. Sargent
        p. cm.
    ISBN 0-8358-9854-7
    1. Bible. N.T. Luke—Meditations. 2. Lent—Meditations 3. Imaginary letters.   I. Title.

BS2595.54.S37 2003
242'.34—dc21   2003009890

Printed in the United States of America

*To the saints in the
Oxford United Methodist Church
Bible study groups.
You helped me learn about imagination.*

✢ CONTENTS

✌ AN INVITATION

Christians traditionally observe Lent by focusing on a specific spiritual discipline. Frequently we give up something. Nearly as frequently whatever we sacrifice corresponds to something that we should give up anyway: chocolate, second helpings, watching television. Thus virtue emerges from necessity. Many years ago I decided to stop watching televised news. I chose instead to use the time for reading, reflection, and writing. I haven't missed the news, and I have written a fair number of letters and read many pages during those otherwise-occupied hours. This book asks you to sacrifice time. That's right, time. Additionally you may find yourself giving up some preconceptions about Jesus and the faith to which we are called. How?

We begin by acknowledging that the stories of Jesus did not originate as anvils on which to forge theological tenets and creeds. The stories of Jesus arose as reports and recollections from real life. People whom Jesus encountered remembered those dramatic moments and told others about them. People who had seen Jesus remembered the incidents of blind persons regaining their sight, crippled persons walking, feverish children recovering and playing again, and paralytics jumping from their beds. People remembered the pithy stories Jesus told. After many years the Gospel writers, Matthew, Mark, Luke, and John, collected these stories and put them into written form. The Gospels were read aloud in worship and were always intended to evoke response. Though centuries have passed since the stories of Jesus were first collected and committed to written form, the Story and stories still evoke responses. This devotional book reexamines the Gospel according to Luke.

I have yearned for a devotional guide that would have some surprise to it. Far too often I find devotionals read like a joke with a punch line I already know. Since the joke no longer surprises me, it lacks real humor. Jesus of Nazareth was not entirely predictable. A sensitive reading of any of the Gospels reveals a Jesus who confounded people at nearly every turn. People do not easily understand his stories. Even the disciples comprehend what he talks about slowly and gradually. I believe Jesus caught people at the moment of surprise. I can see the glint in his eye when he watches people furrow their brows or when crow's-feet appear at the corners of their eyes as they grin with understanding. If it has to be explained, a joke is not a joke. So also with Jesus' stories. If they have to be explained, then they have not accomplished their goal. They are meant not so much to be explained as they are meant to be encountered.

This devotional book allows us to meet Jesus through a fresh perspective, as if for the first time, so that he can surprise us. We will view Jesus from a different angle and in doing so appreciate a lively encounter both with Luke's Gospel and with Jesus. At the outset we should realize that we will not meet a tamed, domesticated, or familiar Jesus. We must remember that as people met Jesus, listened to his stories, heard his preaching, watched him as he healed, and felt the touch of his hands, they interacted with a man whom they had never before met. They knew only what they may have heard as his reputation spread throughout Galilee and Jerusalem. The real Jesus was hardly tamed or domesticated. His stories startled. His healings offended some people. His attitudes toward conventional wisdom evoked strong response. He touched the untouchable and cared for the forgotten. When people saw him they had strong reactions. Some people associated Jesus with scandal and controversy.

How will we encounter Jesus?

We shall approach Jesus through our imaginations. This style may be a new manner of study for some readers. For some the notion of approaching the Bible with imagination may sound peculiar. Some may even feel uncomfortable. We need not feel uncomfortable. Our imaginations are gifts from God. Through our imaginations we recall favorite moments with long-lost friends. We may recall special hours with our children. We may remember and re-create in our mind's eye a leisurely walk along the shoreline of a lake or along a seashore as breakers crashed into the rocks. Just as we can recall events and create pictures, so also can we encounter God. God can approach and apprehend us through our imaginations. This method has long lineage in Christian spirituality.

In the sixteenth century Ignatius of Loyola developed a method of reading the scriptures that employed the imagination. Ignatius first published his *Spiritual Exercises* in 1548. These guides allow a more personal approach to the narration and interpretation of the stories of Jesus. They invite readers to enter into the drama of each story through their imaginations. This method of active, imaginative personal presence in an incident serves as an alternative to listening passively to lengthy explanations and amplifications of the scriptures. Ignatius's *Exercises* direct persons to converse with Jesus (see Week One, First Exercise, Colloquy) or to imagine Jesus suspended on the cross. In another entry Ignatius invites persons to "see with the eyes of imagination" (*Spiritual Exercises,* 141). Ignatius's *Exercises* instruct persons to imagine a place. Through imagination people see synagogues, towns, streets, villages, and animals. In another instruction he asks persons to picture a road from Nazareth to Bethlehem. Consider its length, its breadth, whether it is level or winds through valleys and hills. Imagine the cave. Is it large or small? Is there any light? How is it furnished? The imagination allows us to picture the place and to enter into the drama. Think for a moment of the difference between the following treatments of the same incident.

Luke 4:31-32 reads: "He went down to Capernaum, a city in Galilee, and was teaching them on the sabbath. They were astounded at his teaching, because he spoke with authority." One could study this brief portion of scripture by examining a description of what Jesus' authority means. One might place Jesus' authority in opposition to that of the scribes or Pharisees, for instance. A listener may or may not be moved by such explanations or arguments. On the other hand, if one imagines hearing Jesus speak, what might occur?

Imagine what a tone of authority sounds like. Perhaps you have heard a masterful teacher tell stories. Recall for a moment how your favorite teacher enthralled you when he or she launched into a story. Bring to mind how you felt as your teacher described the surroundings, the drama that took place, the issues at stake, and the risks people faced. Now imagine Jesus telling some of the stories from the Hebrew Scriptures as a part of his teaching. Imagine the tone of his voice. Listen to him as one man in the crowd poses the questions "Jesus, what should we do about the Roman occupation forces? Do we have any chance of freedom again?" Then listen as Jesus tells the story of David and Goliath. Hear Jesus as he begins, "You remember the story of the time when a bully stepped forward from the enemy lines. . . ." Now watch people as they listen to Jesus. No one wants to interrupt. They want to hear him tell the story because there's something special about how he speaks. They do not know how to characterize the way he teaches and the way he tells stories. At day's end, one of the people who had heard him speak says simply, "He speaks with a special authority." Do you see the difference? In the first instance we have an explanation, information that may or may not affect our daily lives. In the second scenario, we have a moment when we allow ourselves to listen to Jesus tell a story. We have allowed ourselves to hear his tone of voice, his inflection, his wonderful way of enthralling people. I call this approach to reading the Bible "an imaginative engagement or encounter" with the scriptures.

Using our imaginations should not pose a problem. Everyone has an imagination. Remember summer days when you lay on your back gazing at the clouds? You saw horses, wild waves, and maybe a face. You remember the sounds made by the cars, trucks, and construction equipment as you played with toys. Dolls conversed with each other for hours. Remember the worlds that unfolded with the familiar words "Once upon a time . . ." We each have an imagination, but we may have forgotten how to imagine or we may have neglected the gift of imagination.

I want to add a personal comment to this invitation into imagination. For many years I taught the Bible. I did the research, read commentaries, examined word origins, and explored what other preachers had done with the same verses. I also knew what each lesson was supposed to teach. I knew the punch line if you will. I knew what the class or group should learn. Thus my teaching became a kind of "twenty questions" to see how quickly the class could reach the conclusion that I had reached. Not surprisingly, over the course of time class size and participation diminished. Much later I realized that people do not want to be told the meaning of a passage of scripture. People want an encounter with the scriptures, an encounter with Jesus, and an encounter with God through their reading. The path to those encounters, both from the reader to the scriptures and from God by way of the scriptures to the reader, passes through the imagination.

After years of frustration I decided to try something different. Instead of directing a group of people to a conclusion, I worked through their imaginations to get them into the stories and into the scriptures. Tentatively at first but then more energetically and enthusiastically, members of study groups used their imaginations, their senses, and their own experiences as means by which to enter into moments of biblical drama. This unconventional approach yielded remarkable results. People who had never before felt free to ask questions suddenly began asking them. The questions may not have been the ones scholars ask. The questions people asked came from their own experiences, their own wisdom gleaned from living, earning a living, raising a family. They began to be able to place themselves in a story as participants, using all their senses through their imaginations. Most of the people with whom I worked had never imagined themselves overhearing an argument between the disciples and Jesus. Many had not imagined how it must have felt to hear one of Jesus' stories and not get the point of it. Few had imagined that an ancient home where someone was desperately ill might look much like a home today where the family's efforts are completely devoted to caring for the sick person rather than keeping the kitchen clean or the living room straightened. Though all of us had been in a home where freshly baked bread cooled on the countertop, few had imagined what Jesus' home might smell like with a loaf of bread cooling on a table that he and Joseph just finished building.

Over the course of the next forty days of Lent, plus Sundays, we will employ our senses of touch, hearing, sight, smell, and taste as we visit villages, wander through city streets, feel the crunch of gravel beneath our feet, and hear the voices of real people. Throughout these days we will actively engage our imaginations. In the process we will seek Jesus so that we too can hear his voice, see his sensitive eyes, and observe his careful touch. We will strain to listen as he whispers into the ear of a madman, as he touches a leper, as he kisses a child, and as he struggles for breath on a Jerusalem hill called Golgotha. We will seek Jesus from different perspectives.

We all receive letters. We read about a friend's experience on vacation or a family member's anguish over a rough decision. This book of devotions is fashioned as a series of letters written by a man named Eli who has heard about Jesus and is interested in Jesus' ministry. Through this collection of letters by a would-be disciple, we may well come to new understandings, new thoughts, new perspectives on Jesus and on our faith. This method of biblical interpretation assumes that no single word captures the entire range of God's mysterious ways. Nor does any word qualify as the final word. The most skilled commentator and novice alike equally need the means of grace that the scriptures provide. Faithfulness consists of the conversation that the scriptures stir up, not in a single voice or conclusion.

How will this guide work?

Each day's reading offers a portion of Luke's Gospel and a letter from Eli to his friend. Through the course of Lent we will read Luke's narrative from the beginning of Jesus' public ministry in Nazareth to the days following his crucifixion. We will look at events in Jesus' ministry through the eyes of a would-be disciple. We will also examine incidents and moments from the unique vantage point of our own experience through our imaginations. In each letter Eli responds to the circumstance and the incident in different ways. He responds with his emotions. He also responds in his thoughts. We will enter into the moment with all our emotions. We will position ourselves in place of one of the characters of the moment. We may find ourselves in agreement with opponents in one moment and in another, feeling impatient or angry. In yet another we may feel the terrible anguish of witnessing unjust acts but being powerless to act. There are no right or wrong emotions or reactions to the stories, incidents, and people involved. Each of us approaches the scriptures with a unique background, unique experiences, unique hopes, dreams, and aspirations. We should expect different responses within varying circumstances.

Suggestions for reflection conclude each day's reading. These suggestions prompt further reflection, interaction, and imagination. Since letter writing shapes this book, you may want to keep a journal of your thoughts, emotions, reflections, reactions, insights, or other responses to either the scriptures or the devotional guidance. An inexpensive notebook or journal serves the purpose. You may want to imitate the method by writing a letter to a friend, developing your own images, thoughts, emotions, and reactions. Allow your imagination to guide.

"Biblical Reflection(s)," which follows each letter, places you in the first century. "Contemporary Reflection(s)" prompts you to apply your imagination in a modern context. This second set of suggestions encourages you to picture Jesus in a present-day setting, encountering people whom you know, people whom you recognize in familiar circumstances.

The letters do not cover all Lukan stories and incidents. You may want to take a story or incident from elsewhere in Luke as the focus for your imaginative encounter with Jesus.

Both individuals and small groups may find enrichment in this book. Be imaginative. Be daring. Be open to the Spirit of Christ. Be open to the movement of the Spirit.

Day 1: Ash Wednesday

🌱 READ LUKE 4:16-30.

My Good Friend,

I must write to you about a most remarkable man. His
name is Jesus. Nazareth is his hometown. As you know,
I have only recently moved to Nazareth. I went to the
synagogue for worship on the sabbath. The congregation
buzzed when Jesus entered with Mary and Joseph. The
man next to me said that Jesus always attends worship.
Our rabbi invited Jesus to read from the prophet Isaiah.
He found Isaiah 61:1-2. In those first moments everyone
was struck by the unusual way in which Jesus read these
verses. As he read, "The Spirit of the Lord is upon me
. . . to bring good news to the poor," he stressed the word
me. Every other rabbi we've ever heard places emphasis
on the phrase *the Spirit of the Lord.*

Quite honestly I felt a bit uncomfortable. I am
accustomed to hearing about the Spirit of the Lord and
the work that needs to be done. However, when a member
of the congregation reads the scripture with a sense of
personal identification, then it can get almost scary.
Why? I have to confess that the urgency Jesus expressed
indicated a sense of his own identity being wrapped up
in the Spirit and the work. I believe he felt himself to be
the one upon whom the Spirit had been placed.

When Jesus finished reading, he continued by offering
his personal interpretation of the scripture. He referred to

stories about Elijah, the widow, Elisha and Namaan, saying that in those days of crisis God had chosen to work with foreigners. Jesus' interpretation of scripture interested me. I would like to have heard more. I can't remember the last time that I heard good news preached or given to the poor. It's been equally as long since prisoners have been set free. I must say that I have never seen a blind man recover his sight!

However, many in the congregation, who had only minutes earlier murmured approval and appreciation for Jesus, just as quickly became incensed. In fact, the congregation got so angry that they wanted to pitch him over the brow of the hill. They became an enraged mob! One or two people sitting near me whispered their discomfort with the crowd's sentiment, but because they were outnumbered they didn't protest. The tension was nearly palpable. Jesus walked out of the synagogue, surrounded by angry people. When they reached the edge of the hill, he turned and faced them down. Any words I write cannot capture the drama of that moment when he deliberately walked through them. The crowd parted as the waters had when Moses extended his hand. Jesus then simply walked away. I confess his interpretation of scripture ranks high on any list of first sermons.

I'll be writing more,

Elí

Biblical Reflections

❧ Imagine the synagogue in which Jesus reads from the prophet Isaiah. Picture the congregation. Where does Mary sit? Joseph?

What do their faces look like when Jesus reads? What do the faces of the congregation look like as they begin to understand what Jesus is saying about foreigners?

- Read Isaiah 61:1-2 aloud. Imagine how Jesus read the same portion of scripture. How do you hear him? What does his voice sound like? What does his voice sound like as he reads the portion where he identifies himself as the one the Spirit has infused?
- Imagine the congregation. How do you picture the people as they become angry as Jesus speaks? What words angered people most?

Contemporary Reflection

For this exercise allow your imagination to roam freely. You may choose the location, the setting, and the cast of characters. Imagine people you know and with whom you are familiar. You may want to create an unusual scene. For instance, you may want to imagine Jesus sitting in a booth at a local restaurant in your town. You may picture him in a storefront church with a sanctuary in an old theater with squeaky chairs. Or you may imagine Jesus sitting in a pew in the church you attend. Picture him standing at the lectern reading from the prophet Isaiah. When he finishes reading, he begins his interpretation. Be aware of that person sitting next to you. Sense him or her stiffen as Jesus begins talking about God caring for foreigners instead of talking about your nation. What is Jesus' tone as he speaks in your sanctuary?

Note your reactions as you followed the suggestions for reflection. Describe any comfort, discomfort, or new insights about yourself or about Jesus in your journal. What implications for your life might come from this encounter with scripture?

Day 2

✌ READ LUKE 4:31-44.

My Dear Friend,

The past few days have been filled with activities. Jesus healed a man in the synagogue, cured a desperately ill woman, and cared for what appeared to be an almost endless flood of people, all of whom were severely afflicted with dreadful ailments. Small wonder that Jesus wanted to get away by himself.

Early one morning when there was but a hint of silver light on the horizon, without telling anyone, Jesus went to a lonely place. Whether he was worn out from the efforts of the preceding days or needed time to himself in order to be ready for the next rush of needs, I could not determine. Enormous numbers of people clamor for his attention. I was not aware of how many families have been afflicted with illness or how many people are demon-possessed.

I can imagine the frustration I would feel if I had a sick child or a desperately ill friend. I'd want some of Jesus' time. That's for certain. But he can't see everyone. He is only one man and the numbers are against him. I overheard a couple with a sick son get angry when they could not get in line in time to see Jesus. I can't blame them. I wish that I could have done something to help.

Other people in line began talking about how they wished they could hire Jesus as their personal chaplain and physician. When they made their suggestion, Jesus would have nothing to do with the idea. No doubt they were offended that he could not stay. He stated that he had to move on to preach and teach in other towns. Some people standing near me whispered that they suspected he was simply making excuses in order to leave!

Today I am impressed that Jesus does not allow people's expectations to confine him. Remember that first sermon I told you about? He offended people by referring to foreigners. Today he refused to be confined to a small area or to a few people.

Another thought occurs to me. As soon as Jesus' reputation spreads and he becomes more famous, the day may come when he no longer preaches good news to the poor or attends to the sick. What if Jesus realizes the kind of fees he could charge? I've not heard anyone who can preach as he does. If I were poor, I'd make certain I heard him soon. How long will it be before he is priced out of the range of the poor, lame, and sick? Who knows, he may end up in Jerusalem in one of the big-city congregations. Then things will be like they've always been. Big money and prestige will dictate who gets the good preacher! I hope for better.

Blessings,
Eli

Biblical Reflection

Imagine standing in line, waiting to see Jesus. You have brought a friend who needs Jesus' healing touch. What friend stands next to you? Can you tell Jesus what the friend's ailment is? What needs to be healed? Remember that Jesus has worked with people all day. He looks weary. Hope for your friend fades. What do you feel when you hear Jesus say, "I must be going to the work of preaching"? How does your friend react?

Contemporary Reflection

The scripture suggests Jesus healed throughout the course of the night. Imagine Jesus in one of the major cities in your state. He ministers on a city street late into the night. Streetlights illuminate the corner. Long lines of people extend around the block. Though dark shadows obscure the storefronts, flickering flames from a fire in a large steel drum illuminate Jesus' face. Look at Jesus' face as he greets each person. What features do you note? Watch the people who have been touched by Jesus. What do you notice in their faces?

Note your reactions as you followed the suggestions for reflection. Describe any comfort, discomfort, or new insights about yourself or about Jesus in your journal. What implications for your life might come from this encounter with scripture?

Day 3

My Good Friend,

I cannot sleep. I shall write to you before retiring for the night. Today I overheard a brief exchange between Jesus and a leper. Something that the leper said lingers in my thinking. The afflicted man said, "If you choose, you can cure me." I first thought, *How can Jesus do anything else?* Surely Jesus is a man who heals. Did the leper attempt to make Jesus feel guilty? Obviously the poor man needed Jesus to heal him. Why couldn't he simply say so? Was he trying to manipulate Jesus? I felt uncomfortable. I wonder how Jesus felt.

Later in the day I thought again about what the man had said. Did he mean to suggest that Jesus did not have the power to cure him? I have seen enough to consider that possibility. Could the man have thought that Jesus had the power but chose not to employ it on his behalf? Could Jesus be a man of loveless power? What an awful thought. That would make Jesus either capricious or a tyrant. Could Jesus be a man of love without sufficient power to do anything? That would make him simply ineffective, irrelevant, or merely sentimental.

For my part I must conclude, at least tentatively, that Jesus has the power but also has to live with limits on what he can do with that power. He cannot do what he wants to do all the time. Even Jesus cannot heal everyone.

If Jesus had all the power and could use it all the time, it seems to me that you and I would not have to worry about assuming any responsibility for the needs of the world. We could simply wait for Jesus to act. It appears that even Jesus has limits on his power at least with respect to breadth if not depth. At the end of the day I am troubled by the thought that Jesus had a decision to make. He had to decide if he would heal the leper. I wonder what the leper expected Jesus to do.

In my previous letter I described how Jesus would not allow himself to be defined by anyone. Today's encounter with the leper underscores that observation. Jesus will not be tamed or otherwise controlled, even by those who need his help the most. People cannot trigger his action. They certainly cannot predict what he will do. By the way, having said all this, I will tell you that Jesus did finally heal the man. He then instructed the man to fulfill traditional expectations. The former leper must seek out a priest and give thanks. I wonder if he found the priest.

Blessings,

Elí

Biblical Reflection

Imagine standing next to Jesus as the leper speaks to him. The afflicted man has sought healing for a long time. He has not touched anyone's hand for so long he's forgotten the sensation of human touch. He hears about Jesus and desperately wants to receive healing. Now he blurts out, "If you choose, you can cure me!" What tone of voice do you hear? Imagine Jesus responding. Perhaps some of the words Jesus spoke that day did not get into the Bible. What else does Jesus say to the man? What tone do you hear? Say the words you think Jesus would say.

Contemporary Reflections

🎋 Doubtless you know someone who has been yearning for healing. Imagine Jesus meeting that person. Your friend feels awkward and does not want to appear presumptuous. Listen as your friend says, "You can heal me if you choose to. Help me, Jesus." What is it that you and your friend want Jesus to heal? What words do you want to hear from Jesus? Say those words. Write those words in your journal.

🎋 According to Luke 5:1-11, the disciples initially balked at instructions Jesus gave them. Think of a project undertaken by your church that resulted only in frustration. Listen to Jesus as he instructs you and the congregation to try again. What does Jesus say? What keeps you from doing as Jesus urges you? How do you feel when you hear Jesus instruct the disciples? What feelings do you notice when you hear Jesus instruct you?

Note your reactions as you followed the suggestions for reflection. Describe any comfort, discomfort, or new insights about yourself or about Jesus in your journal. What implications for your life might come from this encounter with scripture?

Day 4

✎ READ LUKE 5:15-39.

My Good Friend,

Today's events still intrigue me. Some friends of a
paralyzed man brought him to see Jesus. Jesus
acknowledged the friends' great faith. I don't know
whether the paralyzed man had the same faith, but that
seemed irrelevant. Their faith prompted Jesus to heal the
man. I saw the man lurch to his feet and stumble a few
steps. When he got his balance, Jesus said these wonderful
words: "Your sins are forgiven." Forgiveness and
paralysis? I had never considered the two together.

I had always thought that we must ask for forgiveness.
The paralyzed man said nothing at all. I have no idea
what occupied the man's mind or what troubled his soul.
I do know that the man shook his legs and stood up. I
couldn't help recalling some painful memories that have
long haunted me and for which I yearn to hear words of
forgiveness. Though I can walk, I wonder how it would
feel to hear such gracious words. I suspect it would feel as
if my life had been rescued from the grip of bad memories
and curses of wrongdoing.

I'll tell you another thing about forgiveness. When
someone receives forgiveness, the people who have done
the forgiving don't stand off at a distance either physically
or emotionally. Authentic forgiveness runs perilously
close to condoning. I understand, in part, why people

do not want to forgive. Their forgiveness can be misinterpreted as condoning the wrong committed. Why shouldn't the first impulse be to flee, to get away from the offender? Distance eliminates the danger of confusing forgiveness with tacit approval. If we do forgive, then all efforts to keep distance from the wrongdoers end.

Not long after Jesus healed the paralytic, a tax collector named Levi invited Jesus to his home. Everyone knows how contemptible tax collectors are. They make their living off their fellow citizens by gouging them for every penny they can get. Talk about forgiveness: Jesus willingly sat with Levi at his table. I thought at the time that this took great courage on Jesus' part. What if people saw him at that table with Levi? What might they think? Would they confuse Jesus' forgiveness as somehow approving Levi's past? Jesus' willingness to be seen with Levi impressed me. Jesus dared to sit with someone whom others detested.

Quite honestly I wonder how his actions might affect his reputation. If Jesus wants to avoid offending, he needs to watch the company he keeps. During these past few weeks his reputation has spread quickly and thus far has been excellent. However, many luncheons with questionable characters will make Jesus suspect. Still I have been thinking what it would mean if Jesus, fully aware of *my* offenses, were willing to sit with me. I'd love to hear those words, "Your sins are forgiven." Those words would feel like grace—the most welcome words I can imagine. I'd invite Jesus to my house for lunch too.

Yours,
Eli

Biblical Reflections

🐦 Two individuals receive forgiveness from Jesus. Identify someone you would like to take to see Jesus. The person cannot go alone. You will need to take him or her with you. Imagine the crowd around the room where Jesus sits. Walk with your friend. What do you feel? How does your friend feel?

🐦 Assume the character of either the paralyzed one or the tax collector. In either instance your past cripples you. You'd like to hear Jesus speak words of grace and forgiveness, but you can't go alone. Who will go with you? What emotions would stir up as you approach Jesus? What would you say to Jesus?

Contemporary Reflections

🐦 Imagine Jesus waiting for visitors in one of the homes in your town. You can see him through a picture window, sitting in a living room. Anxiously you walk up the front steps and tentatively knock on the front door. As you approach him, he gestures for you to sit down near him. You've not wanted to tell anyone what haunts you. But something about Jesus encourages you to speak openly. In your imagination, what do you tell Jesus? Now listen as he says, "Your sins are forgiven." Afterward, as you walk away, you want to sit with someone. With whom do you want to share the news of forgiveness and what it means to you? Who will stand next to you or sit at the table? Invite that person and Jesus to be at the same table with you.

🐦 Imagine someone you know who needs forgiveness. Picture that person sitting with Jesus for half an hour, pouring out the contents of a troubled soul. You see Jesus smile, touch the person, and mouth the words "You are forgiven." That person now wants someone to sit with you, to take in fully this forgiveness. She or he looks to you, needing to feel reassured. What happens next?

Note your reactions as you followed the suggestions for reflection. Describe any comfort, discomfort, or new insights about yourself or about Jesus in your journal. What implications for your life might come from this encounter with scripture?

First Sunday in Lent

❧ READ LUKE 6:1-11.

My Good Friend,

I want to talk with you today about Jesus and some of his activities on the sabbath. I don't know why Jesus seems to run into trouble on the sabbath. He delivered his first sermon on a sabbath, and it evoked strong response. You recall that the congregation turned into a mob after hearing him speak. On another sabbath he ran up against people who had seen him with the disciples snacking along the way in a grainfield. I sometimes wonder if Jesus tries to tweak the noses of authority. I cannot determine why he seemed intent on ignoring long-held traditions and conventional thinking. I saw him again just the other day on another sabbath.

During the service, Jesus sensed the Pharisees' suspicion. Rather than wait for their challenge, he issued his own. He asked a man with a withered hand to stand up and come forward. I couldn't determine who was more surprised—the man or the Pharisees. Jesus then asked a simple question, "Can acts of goodness be performed on the sabbath?" Jesus had just taken the wind out of his opponents. Predictably the people who argued with Jesus got mad. He had challenged them publicly both by asking the question and then performing the healing. What were they to do? Could they have insisted that Jesus reverse the healing? They could hardly have done that.

This thought occurred to me: Jesus may be wasting his time. He seems to be trying to convince his enemies. He has yet to learn that enemies won't believe you, and you don't have to explain to friends. Why bother arguing? The man struggled with a crippled hand, and now he is healed. Who cares about what can or cannot officially be done on the sabbath? The real work of God's intention must consist of something other than endless debate, rule setting, and discussion. I would go so far as to say that debate and discussion sometimes constitute ways to avoid the difficult task of actually helping people. If we talk about an issue, we may confuse our talk with work. We may call our discussion about the poor the same as involvement with the poor. A debate about what may be done on the sabbath does not mean the same as helping a crippled man on the sabbath. Our words are not always the same as action. I hope Jesus realizes this. I don't understand how Jesus' work can be reduced to debates. He can do so much good. It seems terribly tragic to waste his time and energy. This frustrates me!

I must close,
Eli

Biblical Reflections

🌿 Imagine yourself in worship with Jesus. The service proceeds without incident for a while. Suddenly, without any warning, a troubled person disrupts the hour by insisting that Jesus pay attention to his affliction. Note Jesus' face. What emotions does Jesus show? How does Jesus speak to the troubled man? What does the man's face look like after Jesus speaks to him? Someone in the congregation protests, saying that the service should not have been interrupted. What do you say?

🔊 In fairness to the Pharisees, they might have been working with the poor and crippled all week. Perhaps the Pharisees simply wanted an hour during which they could recover from the week's work by centering their thoughts on God instead of more work. Imagine a moment when a demand from a needy person felt like an interruption to you.

Contemporary Reflection

Jesus seemed unconcerned with matters that were important to Pharisees. Can you think of a time when you too felt resistance to someone who did not seem concerned about an issue you considered important or sacred? In my ministry for quite a long time I felt threatened by those who insisted that the congregation I served be what is known as a "reconciling congregation." I didn't want to endure the controversy, so I reacted by trying to silence the protests. Since that time my attitude has changed, but I remember how animatedly I protested. Jesus upsets norms. What concerns generate controversy or conflict in your congregation? How do you determine which are major and which are minor concerns?

Note your reactions as you followed the suggestions for reflection. Describe any comfort, discomfort, or new insights about yourself or about Jesus in your journal. What implications for your life might come from this encounter with scripture?

Day 5

✎ READ LUKE 6:12-26.

My Good Friend,

My thinking today orbits around two sets of events. First, Jesus made it official today: He selected his disciples. Second, Jesus began teaching specifically for the disciples.

Let me tell you how Jesus selected the disciples. Who qualified? I checked with a man privy to the details. He told me that Jesus prayed the entire night before announcing the names. From what I have seen, large numbers of people are following Jesus. Small wonder, given the nature of the work Jesus has been doing. Jesus performs a miracle or instigates a confrontation. Excitement surrounds Jesus! No one anticipates or predicts what will happen. I know that he intrigues me.

On the day of his announcement, Jesus called people together. His list omitted my name. Frankly I was relieved since I am not quite ready to follow as others seem able and ready to do. Yet the other day, watching Jesus work with the paralytic and tax collector stirred something within me. I want to be near him certainly. Quite honestly I wonder about some of the people Jesus has chosen for disciples. At least one or two seem questionable. The inner circle includes a zealot and a couple of hotheads. Surely Jesus has his reasons for the choices.

Jesus then began teaching about the people who will be blessed. Though some in the group near me nodded their assent, I felt resistance. Jesus spoke in riddles. He spoke of people being blessed by things and circumstances that appeared to me more like curses. I felt very confused. He said, "Blessed are you who are poor, for yours is the kingdom of God." He went on, saying, "Blessed are you who are hungry now, for you will be filled." I thought to myself, *He speaks in contradictions.* A person is either poor or rich, hungry or fed. Don't talk to me about being poor, hungry, and blessed at the same time. Life isn't like that. Imagine how I felt when Jesus continued, "Blessed are you when people hate you, . . . on account of the Son of Man." If accepting these statements amounts to the litmus test for a disciple, then I fall short of the requirements. I don't believe him, can't believe him. Maybe I should soften that a bit: I can't believe him *yet*.

Frankly I wonder what Jesus wants to accomplish. I understand the healings, his preaching, some of his confrontations with authorities. But these blessings confuse me. Do you suppose Jesus continues the prophetic tradition—calling some of us to be different from the surrounding population? If Jesus intends to show how his followers differ from others, then this list of blessings goes a long way toward illustrating just how distinctive they are. Perhaps Jesus waited this long to name his disciples in order to determine who could tolerate his teachings and follow his radical leadership. Who knows how many people want to continue following him after today? These so-called blessings confuse and upset me. They run against the grain of what I hold true. Eventually I want to wrap my mind around this.

I trust this note finds you well.

Eli

Biblical Reflections

🌱 Conventional piety may not allow us to have negative responses to anything Jesus says. However, the assertions of the Beatitudes run against what we experience in life. Imagine yourself sitting next to Jesus on the day he first voiced the blessings. What tone of voice do you hear? What facial expressions does Jesus have? How do you feel as you hear him say these things for the first time? What protests do you wish you could make? In the privacy of a personal conversation, what questions about the Beatitudes would you like to ask Jesus? In your heart of hearts, how do you feel when you hear Jesus say that the poor are blessed?

🌱 Imagine yourself standing next to Jesus as he announces the list of disciples. You may suspect that the list includes your name. What feelings do you have as you anticipate the reading of the names? You note that someone next to you hears her name. How does she respond? What would you like to say to her now that she knows she is a disciple?

Contemporary Reflection

Picture Jesus standing at the door of the food stamp distribution center in a city. A knot of people gathers around him, waiting for the month's allotment of food stamps. Jesus begins speaking. He repeats the Beatitudes. How do people react to him? Jesus says, "Blessed are you who are poor. . . ." What do you feel? What would you like to say to Jesus? How does Jesus react to your question or comment?

Note your reactions as you followed the suggestions for reflection. Describe any comfort, discomfort, or new insights about yourself or about Jesus in your journal. What implications for your life might come from this encounter with scripture?

Day 6

≈ READ LUKE 6:27-36.

My Good Friend,

Many of Jesus' teachings are very difficult to listen to.
Today he spoke about how we should treat our enemies.
I don't need to remind you that few of us like Roman
occupation soldiers.

You can imagine how some people reacted when they
heard Jesus say we should love and pray for our enemies.
They bristled! They did not like being told that they
should pray for those who abuse us. Far too many people
in this area remember how we've been treated.

Later in the day I talked with Jesus about his teaching.
I began honestly. I told Jesus that what he taught sounded
both foreign and uncomfortable. The notion of praying
for my enemies shocks me. My prayer list always includes
family and friends. I don't think I've ever prayed for enemies except in a prayer for relief from oppression and for
removal of the enemy from the territory. When it comes to
people I don't like, I have prayed that they will somehow
change. I've said those kinds of prayers. Jesus listened
patiently. After a while I summoned up the courage to say
what was really on my mind.

I asked Jesus if he truly believed that in a world like
ours his ethics of loving the enemy could work. He
graciously heard my question and protest. He told me
that the day might come when I would be able to see this

practice work. He described an attitude that seemed to me almost impossible to imagine.

Jesus didn't limit his instruction to prayers for enemies. He also included instruction regarding our material goods. If a person needs a coat, we are to give ours. If someone needs money, we should be willing to lend, even if we cannot expect repayment.

I confess that as much as I am intrigued by Jesus and want to believe what he says, this day's teaching disturbs me. I simply cannot accept it, not yet anyway. I have too many memories of enemies who have wished me harm.

I close this note with one further thought. Jesus appeals to me in the sense that his teaching always challenges me. When he teaches, I have to reexamine my assumptions. When he teaches, I cannot easily cling to what I thought and believed previously. He forces me to examine my faith and ethics. He's certainly never dull!

Blessings to you,

Eli

Biblical Reflections

❧ Imagine that you are seated alongside the disciples as Jesus teaches about prayer, enemies, and ethics. You sense strong emotional response among the disciples. What responses do they make? How do they feel as they hear Jesus instruct them to give away their coats and to make loans that may not be repaid? Some people squirm when they hear uncomfortable instruction. Notice how many of the disciples squirm when Jesus speaks about praying for their enemies. What expressions do you see on the disciples' faces?

✤ Imagine that you have a chance to talk with Jesus. You've heard his teaching. A part of you wants to believe that his vision can actually be achieved, but you have reservations. You first ask Jesus where he came up with these radical ideas. How will you ask him? Imagine yourself asking, "Jesus, what made you say that?" Now that you've asked a difficult question, go ahead and ask another difficult question, "Jesus, what makes you certain that your vision can actually work in this world?" He looks at you. Notice his eyes. How does he look at you? Finally he directly into your eyes and speaks. What does he say? What is the source of his inspiration? his hope?

Contemporary Reflection

Imagine going for a walk with a good friend. At length you tell her about a behavior that you've criticized when you see it in another person. Now you suspect that it's your problem as well.

Note your reactions as you followed the suggestions for reflection. Describe any comfort, discomfort, or new insights about yourself or about Jesus in your journal. What implications for your life might come from this encounter with scripture?

Day 7

My Good Friend,

In my most recent letter I told you about Jesus' teaching regarding enemies. Today I have to tell you about something he did. In a word, Jesus showed exactly what he meant. I'm getting ahead of myself. The other day Jesus returned to Capernaum. Frankly I anticipated a few days of relative respite. Up until now Jesus' encounters involved other Jews. Today, however, a most remarkable occurrence took place. A centurion requested that Jesus come to heal his slave. The entire town is abuzz about it.

Most folk in this area still seethe as Roman occupation forces inflict their unjust and cruel rule by force. Most people I know resent the label "Jew boy." We all want to protest, "We have faces, you know." We do not all look alike. Men chafe at commands to carry a soldier's pack for a mile. I've heard any number of people whisper the unmentionable, that the only good Roman is a dead Roman! Thankfully some Roman soldiers treat citizens kindly, and Jewish leaders appreciate them as good Romans.

The tensions that always erupt between Jesus and synagogue leaders were conspicuously absent when Jesus responded to the centurion today. Jesus' comment that he had not encountered such faith in all Israel stunned those who heard it. *Why,* I asked myself, *would Jesus deliberately set up yet another confrontation? Why in Capernaum—a crossroads of commerce and activity?* Does Jesus mean to suggest that people who have been a part of the Jewish tradition cannot embody the faith as much as this occupation army officer? Small wonder that Jesus' words threaten his own people. Quite a few raised their eyebrows and sharply questioned Jesus' comment.

I have to wonder where Jesus' ministry leads. If Jesus embraces the number of radical ideas it appears he will, then he will offend more people. Eventually he may offend everyone! How many people can tolerate his range of concern and compassion? To tell you the truth, today I wonder how his actions and comments affect one of his own disciples, the Zealot.

You see now in my several letters to you how complex Jesus appears. When he embraces the traditions of Moses, the Temple, and the synagogue, people receive him well. At other times he seems almost iconoclastic. He cares for all kinds of people and seems as comfortable with the town character as with the head of the synagogue. I've never met a man like Jesus. I have never met anyone who actually lives the life he teaches about. I have a strong feeling that I can trust him since he lives as he teaches. Jesus truly did love the enemy today.

Blessings to you,

Eli

Biblical Reflections

☙ Assume that a centurion friend asks you to go speak with Jesus for him. You know the rumors about Jesus, but you do not know what to expect. How does Jesus receive you? Jesus responds to your description of the centurion as a good Roman. What does he say? What tone of voice do you hear?

🔖 Assume that you witness the remarkable healing of the centurion's servant. You believe that a friend of yours lives with an equally important need, and you yearn to ask Jesus to help your friend. You know the problem. You prayed for wisdom to help. An opportunity to help presents itself today. You can go to see Jesus. How do you speak to him about your friend? What request do you want to make to Jesus?

Contemporary Reflection

Jesus arrives in your hometown. He eats his lunch at a local restaurant. You know that many people speak evil thoughts about foreigners. The current atmosphere reeks of animosity and distrust. You want to ask Jesus what we should think about people labeled our enemies. Finally you summon the courage to see him. You sit across the table and ask, "Jesus, what should I do?" You feel uncomfortable with popular opinion that berates the enemy or foreigners. You want to know if Jesus feels similar discomfort. Does the accusation of disloyalty or lack of patriotism when one does not berate the enemy bother Jesus? How does Jesus respond? You also want to know how you can resist the popular impulse to condemn and distrust. What do you ask Jesus? As Jesus reaches across the table, he holds your hands in his. He looks intently into your eyes. What does Jesus say?

Note your reactions as you followed the suggestions for reflection. Describe any comfort, discomfort, or new insights about yourself or about Jesus in your journal. What implications for your life might come from this encounter with scripture?

Day 8

READ LUKE 8:26-39.

My Good Friend,

I hesitate making more of this fact than I should.
However, in looking through my notes from the past
few weeks, I see that Jesus seldom mentions by name the
people he heals or helps. People remain anonymous: the
man with a withered hand, the woman of the street, and
the widow's son. Today that changed. I can hardly contain
my excitement as I tell you about this incident.

Jesus had traveled across the Sea of Galilee to the
territory of the Gerasenes. No sooner had he stepped out
of the boat than a raving lunatic ran from a graveyard
toward him. Word was that the poor wretch was homeless
and ran around naked most of the time. He startled me
to the point that I thought I'd jump out of my skin. Had
this lunatic asked me what I had to do with him, I'd have
panicked and said, "Nothing at all!" and fled for my life.
I had no idea what to do, which brings me to what
impressed me about Jesus in this encounter.

When the man asked Jesus, "What have you to do
with me?" Jesus responded calmly. He simply said, "What
is your name?" Jesus' question stopped the man in his
tracks. Evidently no one had ever talked with him in a
normal manner. The madman spoke clearly, "My name is
Legion." Whether that was a street name or his given
name I couldn't tell. Jesus didn't press the issue. The man

called Legion then began talking with Jesus. The man was utterly transformed. He no longer raved. In fact he acted and spoke quite calmly. At first I couldn't tell which was the more miraculous—that Jesus had spoken to the man or that the man had somehow regained his sanity. On reflection, though, I think the real miracle happened when the man understood Jesus' care for him as a person. You see, no one else ever talked with him. No one else had ever wanted to know his name. He'd been known only as "the madman, the lunatic." Jesus wanted to know his name.

I thought about this for a while. In my heart of hearts I know that much of the frantic activity I do is an attempt to quiet the voices of doubt, of self-hate, or of loneliness. Since those dramatic moments when Jesus asked the man's name and then talked with him, I have wished that Jesus would speak to me in similar fashion. If he were to ask my name and then say my name, perhaps I would feel a calming in my soul. That must be part of what happened to the man in the graveyard. I'll tell you this: My initial fright changed into something almost like envy. Jesus changed his life.

I knew something had happened because the man wanted to follow Jesus. Strangely, though, Jesus would not let him follow. Instead Jesus instructed him to remain in that territory. Evidently Jesus wanted someone there who could give firsthand witness to what he had done.

Blessings to you,

Eli

Biblical Reflection

Imagine standing next to Jesus as the madman lunges crazily toward you. You had heard the madman raving from a distance. Jesus does not seem particularly upset. What do you feel? How does Jesus appear to be handling the circumstance? What is his stance? How does Jesus greet the man?

Contemporary Reflections

🌱 Jesus asked for a name. Imagine sitting at a table in a restaurant. Jesus enters, walks to your table, and asks your name. How does he ask? You have a nickname, a given name, and one good friends use. Which name do you give him?

🌱 The story suggests that Jesus met the man in the location where the man needed to be made whole. Jesus encountered the madman in a graveyard. If you could arrange a meeting with Jesus today, where would it take place? Describe that location and how the meeting would go. How does Jesus say your name?

Note your reactions as you followed the suggestions for reflection. Describe any comfort, discomfort, or new insights about yourself or about Jesus in your journal. What implications for your life might come from this encounter with scripture?

Day 9

🪰 READ LUKE 8:40-56.

My Good Friend,

A comment in your most recent letter lingers in my mind. You said that in this vast empire and in our own territory of Judea, we run the risk of being anonymous, unknown, and of no account. You asserted that in some instances it might appear that we never lived at all, that we were never even on the face of the earth. So, you asked, what difference does it make what one person does or says? Today's events may be instructive.

Jesus returned from a brief trip across the lake. People greeted him with great fanfare. Some of the people standing near me commented that the welcome resembled one given to a military commander returning heroically from battle. People in the crowd jostled to get a better view of Jesus. In the midst of it all, Jesus suddenly stopped. He turned and asked, "Who touched me?" The people in his immediate vicinity gasped. They wondered if Jesus had been offended somehow. I heard one person wonder aloud if Jesus would respond arrogantly. He surely doesn't know Jesus. But frankly I was a bit surprised too, and I had no idea what had happened. Why had Jesus stopped so abruptly?

Jesus said he knew someone had touched him because he felt power go out of him. Peter, always the one to speak first, gestured around at the milling crowd. He pointed out that with all the commotion, someone was bound to touch him. During the uncomfortable silence that followed, a woman emerged from the crowd. Frail from years of illness, she shook nearly uncontrollably. Little did I realize that she might have been shaking from sheer delight. When she finally spoke, her voice carried in the afternoon air. She gasped, "I've been healed!" I could hardly contain myself. I gasped too. Then I started crying.

I recalled thoughts that crippled me, of hurts and self-accusation that have echoed for years. For a moment I allowed myself to imagine what it would be like to touch Jesus, to feel the power of God surge into my life. I tried to imagine being healed. What would it be like? What would it feel like to hear Jesus say, "Go in peace"?

So, to get back to your contention that our lives are of no consequence, I remind you of this woman who received power when she touched Jesus' robe. Jesus felt the power leave him. From this I conclude, if only tentatively, that our lives do make a difference. Somehow Jesus knows and cares for individuals. So long as he knows me, I will find courage to act as if my life makes a difference. I will trust that Jesus sees and somehow knows what I am trying to do. After all, to the officials of the empire that woman had been a nameless cipher on the tax rolls. To Jesus she was a person in great need. He noticed her.

I told you earlier that I stood at the edge of the crowd. I am not ready yet to be a follower. But my mind is changing. Something in my soul wants to know Jesus. Something in my soul wants to be known by Jesus.

More later,

Eli

Biblical Reflections

🕿 Look at the woman's eyes. When she sees Jesus at a distance, her eyes widen as she considers what she is about to try. Then, as she shoves her way through the crowd, her eyes narrow and focus intently. She concentrates on his robe. Desperately, at the last second, she lunges to touch Jesus. Surely she didn't expect the entire parade to stop suddenly. She is delighted to be healed. She is also terrified at having been singled out. In your imagination's eye, what do you notice?

🕿 If any one ailment or problem of yours could be healed by touching Jesus, what would it be? What troubles you? Regarding what circumstance would you like to hear Jesus say, "Go in peace"? Imagine yourself standing at arm's length from Jesus. He is facing the other direction, busy with something else. But with a little extra effort you can reach him. You reach and ever so gently touch his robe. He turns to face you. Somehow he knows that power has gone into you. The problem is resolved. Listen as Jesus asks, "Who touched me?" Answer him. Take the time to tell him your name. You feel as if you should describe what troubled you. However, you realize that he already understands. Now, listen as he says to you, "Go in peace." Later that day you say a prayer of thanksgiving. Write that prayer.

Contemporary Reflection

Recall a time when you stood on a curb waiting for the light to change to "Walk." The crowd of people grew as time passed. Recall the sensation of the crowd's growing. Now imagine that same group of people standing at the same curb waiting for Jesus to pass by. As he approaches from your left, you feel movement at your right elbow. A woman seems intent on getting to the front of the crowd. Initially you are impatient, but your intuition tells you she has something important on her mind. She has to see Jesus, and you sense you could help her. Without asking, she grasps your right elbow. You nudge forward saying, "Excuse me," to people. Remarkably they part so that you and the woman can get through. Jesus approaches, and you now feel the same urgency that the woman feels. Just as Jesus arrives at the corner, you and the woman stand within inches of him. She glances at you. You glance at her and then at Jesus. She reaches out to touch his arm.

Jesus stops, looks around. He catches first the eye of the woman and then your eye. Jesus speaks. What does he say to you? What brief word does he say in response to your helping that desperate woman touch him?

Afterward you go back to your home. At the supper table one of your family asks if anything noteworthy happened today. You want to tell them the story of the desperate woman, a crowd of people waiting at a crosswalk, and a chance encounter with Jesus. What will you tell them?

Note your reactions as you followed the suggestions for reflection. Describe any comfort, discomfort, or new insights about yourself or about Jesus in your journal. What implications for your life might come from this encounter with scripture?

Day 10

My Good Friend,

I am trying to capture some of the drama of Jesus' life and ministry in my writing. You must know I could have written about a great deal more! And I'm sure you realize that what I write is from my perspective. If someone else were to write to you, doubtless you would get a different view and hear a different set of perceptions. Each of us sees Jesus differently. Each of us has a particular response to what he says and what he does. I have often thought that if we are to understand Jesus, the two of us should compare our notes, our perceptions, and our thoughts. Then we could see how Jesus speaks to each of us.

Today, for instance, I heard Jesus speak with the disciples. It seemed like a critical moment to me. He authorized them to go out and in essence do what he has been doing. This impressed me for a number of reasons. First, he gave no indication that he wants to keep all power and authority for himself. Second, he trusted his disciples to do the right thing. I wonder if Jesus had been reading the Torah the day he issued these directives. I remember reading the story of Moses' father-in-law in the book of Exodus. Moses had been doing all the judicial work by himself. His father-in-law counseled him to secure assistance because Moses needed help with the day-to-day administration of judgment. Moses would then be able to attend to difficult cases requiring his expertise. I'd say that ancient counsel is good for anyone, even if your name is Jesus. Jesus didn't choose to do all the work by himself.

When the disciples returned, they predictably were flushed with excitement, enthusiasm, and a sense of success. A couple of them appeared to swagger a bit. Impatience energized them.

After a day's services and preaching in Bethsaida, the disciples asked Jesus to send the folks home. Jesus would hear nothing of the sort. Instead he instructed the disciples to feed the people. All the disciples protested! They gave excuses: They did not have enough food, and they did not have means by which to get enough food to feed many people. I was curious how Jesus would react to their protests. He'd given them authority to go out. They'd gone. But then when he asked them to provide for people in the immediate vicinity, the disciples objected. Jesus didn't say much. He simply took a loaf of bread, gave thanks, broke the bread into pieces, and began distributing it. You can imagine how the disciples' faces looked when to their utter amazement the entire crowd enjoyed ample bread! I was surprised too.

I'll conclude with one brief note. When Jesus handled the bread, his gestures and his words stirred me. It seemed as if he gave a part of himself to everyone gathered there. I lost track of the number of people he fed. Everyone who was there will remember that special moment. I wish I could relive it.

Greet your family for me,

Eli

Biblical Reflections

🌱 We've all stood in line. Imagine yourself standing in line waiting for your turn to receive a piece of bread from Jesus. What do you notice about Jesus? How does he look at each person who stands in front of him? Notice how he breaks off a piece of bread for everyone. Notice his hands as he places a piece of bread into waiting hands. Notice how he leans forward to whisper something to each person. What would you like Jesus to say to you as you receive your piece of bread?

🌱 You've heard grace, waited your turn, and received the piece of bread. Now, allow yourself to taste the bread, a large enough piece that you take several bites. All kinds of grains have been used to make it. Note its consistency. How does it taste?

Contemporary Reflection

Imagine Jesus authorizing you to go out to do the kind of work he did during his time on earth. Where do you imagine yourself going? What part of his work most excites you? What part of the work scares you?

Note your reactions as you followed the suggestions for reflection. Describe any comfort, discomfort, or new insights about yourself or about Jesus in your journal. What implications for your life might come from this encounter with scripture?

Second Sunday in Lent

🌿 READ LUKE 7:11-17.

My Dear Friend,

An incident I haven't shared with you has forced its way into my thinking. I haven't known what to do with it, and I'm not certain my words will be adequate to describe it and my response. Nevertheless, I must try to tell you about an event that both thrilled and frightened me. You may find this hard to believe. Trust me, it was equally difficult for me to believe what I saw with my own eyes.

Jesus went to a town called Nain where he came upon a funeral procession. Men carried the body of a widow's son. The absolutely grief-stricken widow had only this one son. She faced living alone for the rest of her life. I could only imagine her grief compounded by her loneliness. The whole scene saddened me to the point of silence. I could think of nothing to say. No one could. You can well imagine, then, how Jesus shocked all of us when he spoke to the woman, "Don't cry." Don't cry?! Silently I wondered to myself how Jesus could have said such a thing. Had he lost all touch with reality? Did he not realize how deeply the woman grieved and how incredibly desperate her life had become? I didn't dare look at Jesus for fear that he would see my shock and dismay at his apparently cavalier attitude.

Then he did something no one could have anticipated. He went to the bier and touched it. I thought my heart would pound out of my chest. The men carrying the body stood as still as pillars. Then Jesus spoke, "Young man, get up and walk." One woman near me whispered sharply, "Has he lost his senses?" But before anyone could say anything else and before any of us realized what had happened, the corpse sat up! I thought I would pass out. Nothing in my experience had prepared me for what happened on that street right in front of my eyes. I still don't know what to say.

The woman stood dumbfounded at first and then became nearly hysterical with joy as her son blinked his eyes as if waking from an afternoon nap. She tried to talk but couldn't. She tried to say thank you but couldn't form the words. She could only say, "Oh, Jesus . . . Oh, Jesus . . . ," as she sobbed, still in half-disbelief.

People around me gasped. A few couldn't contain themselves. They exclaimed, "I can't believe what I just saw. I just can't believe this!" After a few minutes I heard one person express what we all felt. He said, "A great prophet has risen among us." I almost hesitate saying this, but I must. It appears to me that Jesus has the power of life. As crazy as this may sound, I believe he may have the power to bring the dead back to life. You may think I have taken leave of my senses, but I saw this with my own eyes. It happened in Nain. People can't stop talking about the dramatic events of that day.

I must close,
Eli

Biblical Reflection

Probably everyone reading this book has attended a funeral. You have followed the hearse to the cemetery and walked slowly behind the pallbearers as they carried the casket to the grave. Imagine standing with Eli as Jesus approaches the grief-stricken woman. What do you expect Jesus to do? What words of comfort and assurance will he offer to this desperate woman, now alone? What do you want to hear Jesus say?

Contemporary Reflection

Imagine the shock that went through that gathering as the young man sat straight up and blinked his eyes. Now imagine Jesus speaking to a circumstance that seems as unfixable to you as that young man's death seemed irreversible to his mother. What circumstance do you describe? Listen for what Jesus says about this circumstance.

Note your reactions as you followed the suggestions for reflection. Describe any comfort, discomfort, or new insights about yourself or about Jesus in your journal. What implications for your life might come from this encounter with scripture?

Day 11

🐦 READ LUKE 9:51-62.

My Good Friend,

Thank you for your kind letter. You mentioned a time
when you heard Jesus speak words of forgiveness. You
went on to say how good that moment felt. I can only
dream of that right now. You see, I still feel as if I'm at the
edge of the crowd. Quite honestly I have been wishing
lately that I could follow him.

Galilee proved to be a remarkably lively territory.
Many people clustered around Jesus. The other day,
however, Jesus made the decision to leave the comfortable
confines of the north. In preparation for the journey he
sent disciples ahead, evidently to make arrangements for
housing along the way. Almost as soon as the journey
began though, arrangements began falling apart. The
reasons people gave for refusing Jesus were vague. I heard
a couple of people say that they didn't appreciate Jesus'
decision to go to Jerusalem. The disciples' reactions
bothered me. They were ready to punish every one of the
inhospitable people. Indeed, the disciples initially sought
to rain fire on all the offenders.

In matters of religion, disciples seem quick to wish
harm on anyone who doesn't agree with them or welcome
them. I had heard of this, but I'd not seen it close up.
Therefore, when the disciples approached Jesus to tell him
their thoughts, I was curious to see what Jesus would do.

The longer I watch Jesus, the more I respect what I will call his essential integrity. I now recall hearing Jesus give instructions at the beginning of the disciples' work. He told them if they were welcomed, then they should stay; if they were not welcomed, then they should shake the dust from their heels and move on to the next town. That's easy enough to talk about, but in the pressure of the moment, it would be very difficult to pull off. I can see that Jesus is a man of his word. When he heard the disciples' threats, he faced them down with an intensity that I'd not seen before. Jesus spoke tersely, saying that he absolutely would not tolerate such talk. Later, after that blistering challenge, one disciple told me he'd understood Jesus to say he had come not to destroy lives but to save them. What he meant was not entirely clear to the disciple. Jesus will not lift a hand against his opponents.

I had a flight of imagination the other day. You know what would be ironic? What if people who follow Jesus forget what Jesus has said about opponents? Do you suppose the time might come when disciples would actually do harm to others in the name of Jesus? Could there come a time when disciples would confuse their own anger with the intentions of Jesus? Pray to God this never happens.

Yours,

Eli

Biblical Reflection

Imagine standing with Jesus as he knocks at the door of a home, his anticipated lodging place for the night. Through a partially open door the man inside refuses to let Jesus in. He mutters, "No vacancy," and closes the door. What does Jesus say now? With what tone of voice does Jesus speak?

Contemporary Reflection

Imagine seeing Jesus approach you. You have something that you want to keep secret. At the same time, you have heard that when people talk to Jesus and hear him speak, whatever has disturbed them somehow seems less threatening. Thus you want both to flee and to remain. Anxiously you look around to see where you could go in order to avoid Jesus. But you don't flee. You choose to stay. The tension inside you builds. What issue stirs such strong internal conflict? Now you can understand why some people don't want to encounter Jesus. An encounter with Jesus may mean an encounter with yourself. For what issue in your life might Jesus offer a healing word?

Note your reactions as you followed the suggestions for reflection. Describe any comfort, discomfort, or new insights about yourself or about Jesus in your journal. What implications for your life might come from this encounter with scripture?

Day 12

❧ READ LUKE 10:1-37.

My Dear Friend,

Jesus has done it again. Hoping to catch him off guard, a man asked Jesus a loaded question, "What must I do to inherit eternal life?" Jesus' response was brief. "What is written in the law?" he asked. The man answered, "You shall love the Lord your God with all your heart, and with all your soul, and with all your strength, and with all your mind; and your neighbor as yourself." He might well have added that all the rest is commentary.

Wouldn't you know it? Jesus went on to describe the "neighbor" by posing a Samaritan as the heroic character. A Samaritan, of all people! You'd think that after the near riot in Nazareth following his first sermon, Jesus would be more cautious in his comments.

By my reckoning, thus far in his ministry Jesus has talked about or managed to come into contact with just about every unwelcome, despicable, and otherwise unlikable character imaginable. Moreover he has treated every one of those characters as welcome friends. In some instances he seemed to admire them! I do not understand Jesus. He seems to go out of his way to frustrate or anger people. If Jesus cares about finding people to follow him as disciples, he should be more guarded in his ways and be a good deal less confrontational. My question is this: Why does Jesus, who seems on the one hand to want followers, continually illustrate his stories with foreigners and other questionable individuals?

Now that I've started, I might as well finish. The other day I heard Jesus tell would-be followers that foxes have holes and birds have nests as safe havens. Then he cautioned others that they would be like a lamb in the midst of wolves. Why does he caution people? Would anyone choose to be homeless or constantly in peril? I wonder if Jesus expects to attract any followers.

On second thought, however, I suspect that Jesus is not primarily concerned with gathering a large following. Nor is he interested in being an "answer" man. He refuses to give easy answers: He always forces people to make their own decisions.

I will say one thing: Jesus will end up in Jerusalem. As to what will happen when he gets there, I have no idea. Mystery shrouds future events. I have come this far with him and been challenged practically every day. I feel more alive than I ever felt before meeting him, and I'm going to stay with him. Even when he speaks in riddles, I sense a peculiar liveliness in his thought—and in mine.

Every blessing to you,

Eli

Biblical Reflections

❧ Familiarity with Jesus' parables prevents our being offended by the illustration centering on a Samaritan. We may also run the risk of losing the offense of the gospel. Imagine yourself being able to sit down with Jesus, away from the other disciples. Imagine yourself sitting with Jesus in the shade of a palm tree. The dust from the street swirls, flies buzz. In this homely setting you see a moment when you can be honest, when Jesus will reveal a little more of his feelings and personal thought. How does Jesus feel about the threat of persecution or death? How does he regard his compelling warning about the cost of discipleship? What part of his preaching does he find most difficult?

🌱 In Luke 10:21-22 Jesus says a prayer. Imagine yourself with Jesus—again away from the crowd. The two of you have been quiet for a while. You've been working up your nerve to ask him to do you a favor. You would like to hear Jesus say a prayer just for you. He wants to hear your request. His prayer will not be a generic prayer this time. This prayer will lift up your name and your concern. What will you ask Jesus?

Contemporary Reflection

Jesus spoke favorably of a character who most listeners considered despicable. Bring to mind a person from an ethnicity other than your own about whom you have heard prejudicial remarks. Cast that person in the role of the Samaritan. Imagine telling this story to a group of friends. Tell the story in such a way that two other characters, more acceptable to your friends, avoid contact with the beaten man. You conclude the story with the less-acceptable character as the hero or heroine. This exercise may take some time and will stretch your imagination.

Note your reactions as you followed the suggestions for reflection. Describe any comfort, discomfort, or new insights about yourself or about Jesus in your journal. What implications for your life might come from this encounter with scripture?

Day 13

❧ READ LUKE 11:1-28.

My Good Friend,

As I suspected, tensions, confrontations, and conflict escalate. The grand days in Galilee seem long past now. I must slow down. I'm getting ahead of myself.

The disciples do not ask for much. Jesus has bestowed upon them a great deal already: authority to preach, teach, and heal. They possess the privilege of talking with Jesus regularly. I've often thought that I would like to talk with someone truly wise. I have no interest in talking with someone who is so heavenly minded that he is no earthly good. Jesus manifests that wisdom and depth for which I yearn. I'd like to talk more about life with Jesus.

The other day one of the disciples spoke for the entire group when he asked Jesus to teach them how to pray. They knew that Jesus prayed before every major decision, and they had observed him go off to be by himself frequently. They had also seen John the Baptist teach his disciples how to pray. Now Jesus' disciples wanted to know how he prays.

From what I gathered, Jesus gave them a kind of classic Jewish prayer. The simplicity of Jesus' prayer strikes me. I can remember it. My task now is to pray the prayer as mine! First, by addressing God as "Father," Jesus acknowledges God as Creator and sustainer of the world. I welcome this opening thought because it provides a corrective to the claims of the empire that Caesar is god. Next Jesus prays for the intention of God to be accomplished in the world. The following segment of his prayer causes me to reflect. You see, I have always taken my daily ration for granted. My table always has food on it. Jesus includes an acknowledgment that God provides the daily portion we need. When he said that part of the prayer, it sounded almost like a blessing before a meal. The next segment won't surprise you at all since I have told you how many times the theme of forgiveness crops up in Jesus' teaching and ministry. He prayed for forgiveness, but he added a kind of reflection. We are to be forgiven only as we forgive. As for the final segment, I still wrestle mightily with temptation. Oh my, do I pray to be delivered from evil and the tempter!

I doubt that Jesus intends for us to say these exact words all the time. It seems to me that this prayer serves as an outline of what to include in prayer. In essence he has revealed to the disciples how he prays.

You may not realize this, but Jesus has little tolerance for sentimentality as a replacement for real religion. A large number of people follow Jesus. The more he teaches his stringent demands, the more I wonder if he ever intended to garner a large following. Jesus always refers to the Torah, the Prophets, and the Writings. He has enormous insight into the traditions of our people. Yet he forever challenges our assumptions and our thinking. However, I think he challenges us in order to prevent our following blindly or blandly. Jesus seems to be trying to live out the highest calling of God. I wonder how many people can understand him, much less live the life to which he summons us. I know this: No one I know lives as radically as he does.

One closing thought: Wouldn't it be ironic if people who follow Jesus forgot that his prayer is essentially a Jewish prayer? Wouldn't it be something if people overlooked the fact that Jesus is Jewish and radically so at that? I cannot imagine that happening.

Blessings to you,
Eli

Biblical Reflections

🌱 Imagine sitting with Jesus and the other disciples. You have heard him instruct the disciples about what prayer might include. You have been listening to Jesus' explanation and description of prayer. As he says each phrase, you want to interrupt him with your questions. Imagine saying, "Jesus, when you say that, what comes to your mind?" What does Jesus reply? To which parts of your life do his words point?

🌱 As Jesus explains his prayers and indicates where in your life you might want to spend time in reflection and prayer, you probably know at least one area you'd rather avoid or ignore. What portion of your life do you want to protect against Jesus' prayers? Perhaps, as Jesus speaks, you sense one particular arena of your life now opening to Jesus. What do you want to open up to him?

Contemporary Reflection

Imagine that you are seated with Jesus. He says to you, "Let's go for a walk." You finally have half an hour with Jesus—time during which you can open your soul to him. Where do you walk? Feel the surface of the path beneath your feet. Listen to the crunching of gravel or rustle of leaves on the path. Listen to the sounds of the day: birds singing, water flowing in a stream, a breeze whispering through the trees. You finally have found the strength to confess to Jesus, "I wish that I knew God's will for my life." Jesus walks with you for a few more yards and finally responds. What does Jesus say to you? What do you want him to say? To what aspect of your life do you want to hear him speak?

Note your reactions as you followed the suggestions for reflection. Describe any comfort, discomfort, or new insights about yourself or about Jesus in your journal. What implications for your life might come from this encounter with scripture?

Day 14

🐟 READ LUKE 11:29-12:3.

My Dear Friend,

I apologize for such a long hiatus in writing. I have been caught up in events of the past few weeks and as a result, simply haven't had time to sit down and compose a letter.

I mentioned the tensions that have erupted between Jesus and the Pharisees. I probably should qualify my comments since I am becoming one of Jesus' followers. I am sympathetic toward Jesus and his work; to Jesus' followers the Pharisees have become problematic. However, I am enough a historian to see where the conflict originates. We have misunderstood and misrepresented the Pharisees. Be patient with me as I try to explain.

Had it not been for the pharisaical movement, we might not have survived as a people. You've heard me argue for this historical context previously. Back in the days when our ancestors could easily have lost their identity and simply vanished, the Pharisees, a lay renewal movement, brought a kind of back-to the-scripture-and-tradition emphasis. They wanted to stiffen the resolve of people who were tempted to give up their identity as Jews; therefore, they emphasized scripture and learning. They also insisted on observance of traditions. In my opinion, many who attempt to excoriate them are setting up straw men. I have always valued tradition. You know that. We've talked about the importance of keeping certain traditions.

I am not surprised when the Pharisees get angry with Jesus' criticism that they are tradition-bound and perhaps a bit arrogant in their attitude. Jesus threatens them. After all, it sounds as if Jesus is ready to do away with precisely what they regard as the source of Jewish identity and life itself. We cannot live in chaos. We must have law and order. Keeping order facilitates life, as illustrated by careful preparation for meals according to cultural patterns. I'd rather see elaborate preparation for a meal than no preparation at all. The same follows for observance of tradition and honoring scripture. I must confess I have moments of agreeing with the Pharisees.

Remarkably, Jesus and the Pharisees seem to agree on some important points. Clearly both favor lay involvement in the life of the synagogue and faith. None of Jesus' disciples come from an aristocratic background. He also believes in resurrection, as do the Pharisees. Why then such huge conflict? If Jesus and Pharisees share these common views, why do they appear so far apart from each other? Again, from my perspective, it seems Jesus gets frustrated with precisely the people in whom he sees the greatest potential. The Pharisees understand the *how* of religion, but they don't understand the *why*. If only Jesus and the Pharisees could talk with one another and quit arguing all the time.

Yours,
Eli

Biblical Reflection

One of the easiest emotions to imagine when Jesus argues with Pharisees is anger. But what if Jesus simply debates? Imagine Jesus having a conversation with someone. They debate the importance of one particular point. Jesus tries to describe the difference between the Pharisees' attitude and what he envisions. How does Jesus' tone of voice sound?

Contemporary Reflection

Scribes and Pharisees get very bad press in the New Testament. Yet some of their views appeal to many contemporary Christians. Hearing someone belittle a tradition that we hold dear hurts us. Imagine hearing Jesus criticize a practice or belief you have always considered critical to your faith. How do you feel when he says, "A person does not have to say that phrase [or practice that discipline or dress in that way] in order to be a Christian"? How does it feel when you hear him criticize one of your traditions?

Note your reactions as you followed the suggestions for reflection. Describe any comfort, discomfort, or new insights about yourself or about Jesus in your journal. What implications for your life might come from this encounter with scripture?

Day 15

❧ READ LUKE 10:29-37.

My Good Friend,

Though I've written about the incident previously, I want to revisit an experience. The other day someone asked, "Who is my neighbor?" Rather than launch into an explanation or description, Jesus told a story. Let me tell you what he said.

The hero of the story was a Samaritan. When he told the story, I heard one man next to me mutter something about Jesus' loyalties. You should have heard the murmur when he recounted how two of our people—the priest and the Levite—failed to help. The ne'er-do-well Samaritan turned out to be the hero. I am grateful for Jesus' story. Jesus spoke kindly of an outsider. We do have that tradition of the righteous Gentile, you know.

Remember the story of Jeremiah, thrown into a cistern and abandoned there. The Ethiopian eunuch Ebed-melech asked permission to rescue the prophet from the dank cistern. The eunuch secured a length of line and rags from the royal waste bin. He lowered the rescue line to the mired prophet and gave a mighty heave. That Ethiopian eunuch—that black man, that non-Jew, that Gentile— rescued Jeremiah. You also remember that after two generations of exile, the prophet Isaiah employed the tradition of the righteous Gentile in his account of the Persian emperor Cyrus, a Gentile, granting release to the captives. At one point the prophet calls Cyrus "his anointed." Yet when Jesus employed the same righteous Gentile tradition, people were surprised and angered. Do you suppose Jesus had been reading the stories of Jeremiah and Isaiah the day he told this story?

I can appreciate how the people became frustrated when Jesus, the visiting rabbi, pointed to a Gentile as a hero. He seemed to be ignoring our own people. Why couldn't he have told about a good Jew? It seems Jesus always sees the essential humanity in people. He does not notice what makes people different. Frankly I wonder if Jesus even sees a foreigner! He sees what makes people similar. He pays attention to people's feelings, their need to be known, their need for forgiveness.

One more thing. I tend to characterize Jesus' stories as humor. Why? Humor happens when a story ends differently than we expect. The punch line falls so far from what people foresee that their faces show surprise when they hear it. What is more surprising than hearing about a hero from the other side? When you think about it, most of Jesus' stories come to a conclusion at odds with what we anticipated when he began the story. I know I am surprised practically every time.

The day may come when any notion of scandal or controversy swirling around Jesus is lost. I like his different approach. Jesus' compassion feels good. He appeals to me. His stories include memorable characters. I hope Jesus keeps his stories sharp, with an edge. They challenge my thinking, and I confess a kind of pleasure in watching people squirm when they hear these stories.

Blessings to you,

Eli

Biblical Reflection

Jesus is a consummate storyteller. Like all good storytellers, his sense of timing is excellent. Imagine Jesus telling the story of three characters and a man in need. Jesus describes the two Jewish characters according to their official functions. He describes the Samaritan by his attitude and behavior. Jesus envisions "the other" as fully human.

Listen to Jesus again. Sit with him as he tells the story. Imagine other people listening. One of them attempts to interrupt Jesus. Look at Jesus' eyes. Watch him as he raises his hand in mute protest, as if to say, "Hear me out."

Jesus has put a compassionate human face on the outsider. Tell Jesus how that feels to you. Ask him how he came up with that insight.

Contemporary Reflection

Think for a moment of individuals whom your church does not welcome. At this point you must be brutally honest with yourself. For all the talk of welcome, forgiveness, and compassion, there are still people who would not be genuinely welcome at next Sunday's church supper. Now imagine Jesus using precisely one of those individuals as a hero while the preacher and lay leader are described as failures. How do you feel when you hear that? How does that story play if Jesus tells it to the congregation during questions and answers after the sermon?

Note your reactions as you followed the suggestions for reflection. Describe any comfort, discomfort, or new insights about yourself or about Jesus in your journal. What implications for your life might come from this encounter with scripture?

Day 16

❧ READ LUKE 12:13-34.

My Dear Friend,

For anyone with even modest discernment, Jesus delivered a clear message the other day. A man approached Jesus and asked him to settle a family dispute. The man and his brother disagreed on how to settle the family estate. He asked Jesus to be an arbiter, to decide for them. Jesus refused, saying something to the effect that he would not judge between two brothers.

I've been thinking about that situation ever since. Why would the man make Jesus responsible for a decision that he and his brother couldn't reach? Also I have wondered why Jesus refused to give a specific answer. Then I realized that Jesus did not want to take sides with one man against the other.

It bothers me that some people want Jesus' assistance in taking sides against someone else. Two-to-one odds defeat one person. I've listened to Jesus long enough to know that even if he did have an opinion about which man had the greater claim to the family wealth, he would not have given any indication. Only his unpredictability is predictable, yet some people still believe they can anticipate what Jesus will say or do. He remains elusive and hard to categorize.

Perhaps I should state one thing that Jesus can be counted on to say: Wealth of any sort does not impress him. The story he told, at first blush, apparently missed the point of the brother's question. However, the rich man's concern for larger storage barns stirred something in me. I don't know how that brother felt about the story, but I felt very self-conscious. Wealth concerns me.

Later I sat with Jesus and asked some questions. I understood the farmer who wanted to augment his holdings. Jesus raised his eyebrows, drew a breath, and said to me, "No possessions warrant rupturing a family." My face flushed with embarrassment. I have a lot to learn if I am to move from the edge of the crowd toward being a disciple. Jesus was patient. He didn't seem frustrated at all. He treated my question and concern with great care. In a very gracious way he told me that the story is about priorities. If we were to get our priorities straight, we would have much better relationships. Money would not be the problem that it is. Since he lives in a way consistent with what he teaches, I had to believe him. The only words I could muster were, "Thank you. Please be patient with me."

Blessings to you,

Eli

Biblical Reflection

Picture the two brothers in this incident. One of them runs out of patience and goes to see Jesus. Imagine that you are the other brother. What do you expect Jesus to say to your brother? What emotions surge within you as you watch your brother walk away from you to find reinforcement for his way of seeing things? What would you like to say to Jesus?

Contemporary Reflections

🌿 For what decision confronting you would you want to request Jesus' arbitration?

🌿 When Eli missed the point of Jesus' central concern, he felt embarrassed. Imagine yourself sitting with Jesus. The thought that perhaps something you own, or want to own, interferes with a relationship bothers you. Everything in you wants to tell Jesus, but embarrassment prevents you. Red-faced and hesitant, you build up the nerve to say it. Look into Jesus' eyes. What do you see? Look at his hands. Imagine that he reaches toward you in a gesture of invitation. He holds your hands in his. How do his hands feel? What body language do you notice? Listen to Jesus speak. What does he say to you after you've dared confess?

🌿 After you have told Jesus your secret, you confess that you would like to hear one more word from him. You need to feel a burden lifted from your soul. Tell Jesus how you are feeling right now and wait for his response, which could be a sound, a word, an image, a silence.

Note your reactions as you followed the suggestions for reflection. Describe any comfort, discomfort, or new insights about yourself or about Jesus in your journal. What implications for your life might come from this encounter with scripture?

Third Sunday in Lent

READ LUKE 12:35-48.

My Good Friend,

Jesus told some stories the other day that upset me. These stories, about lamps and servants, focus on end time. I confess that the topic of the end of time usually leaves me completely cold. I just excuse myself from such discussions. Today I heard a conversation among Jesus and some of the disciples. I thought I could listen without participating. But the conversation upset me, and I got involved.

I think the disciples had asked for clarification and explanation about the end of time. Peter wanted to know if Jesus' story about having the lamps lit and being servants ready for their master was for the disciples or everyone. Wouldn't you know it—Jesus turned around and asked what the disciples thought he meant! It seems to me that Jesus was not all that concerned about the end of time—certainly not as much as other religious types. When Jesus prevailed on me to join the conversation, I suggested that he is concerned more with what happens this side of judgment than what follows judgment.

I felt uncomfortable trying to put thoughts into words. I tried to say that a number of people feel no direct consequence of their actions. The Roman emperors always bend the truth; therefore, the people never believe anything the emperor says. It's tragic people don't expect to hear truth from the emperor. If any emperor had realized this would be the consequence of his actions, perhaps he would have changed his ways. Lying brings its inevitable consequences; truth telling also brings its results. I asked Jesus if I was on the right track. He answered, "You are speaking of consequences and the undetermined time of their coming, right?"

I concluded by saying that if we could see the moral consequences of what we do within a short period of time, we might be better off. Some consequences emerge so far distant that we don't see them at all. We lose connections between action and consequence.

It follows that since we cannot see the consequences of our own behavior, we blame consequences on someone else. Since there are consequences, Jesus tries to make people realize that the consequences of their behavior may come sooner than they'd anticipated.

One of the disciples seemed confused. He said to Jesus, "Why do you always teach with questions?" Jesus asked him, "What's the matter with questions?" If only Jesus would give us one straight answer, one definitive statement, this business of faith would be a lot easier. I will never understand Jesus' elusive manner. I have this sneaking suspicion that Jesus wants us to be able to live with our own faith, our own thinking, and our own decisions.

Blessings to you,

Eli

Biblical Reflections

🌿 Imagine yourself sitting alone with Jesus. You feel very fortunate for the moment. You think you understand the meaning of his parables about preparedness. However, your uncertainty pushes you to check with him. In your heart of hearts one potential consequence scares you. Thus Jesus' urgency brought you discomfort. What one consequence concerns or scares you?

🌿 When Jesus talks about the end of time and about moral urgency you may feel uneasy. You want to say something to Jesus about what makes you feel uneasy. What do you say to Jesus? How does he respond to you?

Contemporary Reflections

🌿 Jesus' stories convey a sense of urgency. What sorts of things would you like to hear Jesus address to clear your thinking about matters in your life?

🌿 You have been forming a question and finally are ready to ask Jesus, "Is this parable meant for one person, or did you mean it for everyone?" Jesus pauses for a moment. Then he draws his breath to speak. How do you feel as you await his response? What do you expect him to say? What will you say if he indicates that this parable of preparedness affects especially you today?

Note your reactions as you followed the suggestions for reflection. Describe any comfort, discomfort, or new insights about yourself or about Jesus in your journal. What implications for your life might come from this encounter with scripture?

Day 17

❧ READ LUKE 13:1-35.

My Dear Friend,

I must start my letter by telling you that frustration places me just this side of angry today. Why do some people try to make all events fit into their way of thinking? Some occurrences just don't fit. Some things just defy a quick explanation. Let me describe what happened.

A knot of people confronted Jesus with a question that stemmed from two tragedies. The first tragedy resulted from another of the governor's excesses. In yet another attempt to quell a revolt and to frighten the populace into submission, the governor executed some Galileans and then had their blood mixed with a religious sacrifice. In the second tragedy, a tower accidentally collapsed, leaving several people dead.

People want an explanation, but how can anyone make sense of this kind of thing? Why waste a rabbi's time trying to explain the unexplainable? Do people believe an explanation exists for everything? Can Jesus be expected to have a theological interpretation for every event that crashes down on people? Can't accidents happen without theological interpretation? Does God remain responsible for everything? I didn't hear the entire conversation, but I imagine at least one person said, "How can God remain silent when such horrors happen?" Such a question puts the rabbi in the difficult position of having to defend God.

To his credit, Jesus didn't take the bait. He as much as said that God does not make all events happen. Some events seem to have a life of their own. We may not like it, but reprisals do take place; people die in accidents. There exists no further explanation.

I appreciated the fact that Jesus didn't stop there; he went on to say that unless people put their lives in order, they'd be just as dead as any of those victims. I've thought about that a great deal ever since. Do you suppose he meant it literally? I suppose people may make decisions or do something that makes a shipwreck of their lives. In those instances I guess the people are, in some ways, just as dead as victims of war or accident. If a person decides to break a law, that individual may find his or her life turned upside down. I've known a couple of people who have made such decisions and speak of their mistakes as a kind of death. Once a decision is made, an irretrievable future whirls into motion, which may signal the death of something. Jesus' keen words definitely silenced those people.

I understand these are weighty topics. I don't intend to make this letter a heavy one. Nevertheless, Jesus' insights and cautions cause me to think seriously about my life. Maybe I don't need to have an explanation for everything.

Blessings,
Eli

Biblical Reflections

✺ You overheard the discussion about repentance. Since then, you have formulated questions about repentance. In fact, you would like to divulge to Jesus the issue you're struggling with. You suspect that the wrong decision could make a shipwreck of your life. You hope Jesus can offer some insight. What would you want to say to him?

✎ The parables of the fig tree (13:6-9), the mustard seed (13:18-19), the leaven (13:20-21), and the narrow door (13:24-30) address in part the disciples' attempts to respond to the calling of faith. In your heart of hearts you harbor reservations. As much as you'd like to believe and exercise your faith, you find it difficult. Imagine listening to Jesus tell these brief illustrations. Everything in you wants to agree while at the same time, everything in you wants to protest, saying, "I don't even have that much faith, Jesus. At least not now." How does Jesus respond to you? What tone of voice do you hear in Jesus' response? What gestures does he make?

Contemporary Reflection

You summon the courage to tell Jesus that you desire more faith. Jesus asks if you would like to pray. At long last Jesus says a prayer for you and your faith. Listen as Jesus prays for you. He says your name, and he says the words you have just told him. His words stir your soul. You say *yes* to something that you have sensed in Jesus. What in Jesus inspires you to say yes to him? Imagine speaking to Jesus at the end of his prayer. You want to tell him, "Jesus, something about you makes me want to have more faith." Say those words. Watch his eyes and hands. Describe his gestures.

Note your reactions as you followed the suggestions for reflection. Describe any comfort, discomfort, or new insights about yourself or about Jesus in your journal. What implications for your life might come from this encounter with scripture?

Day 18

🐟 READ LUKE 14:7-14.

My Good Friend,

In my previous letters I mentioned miracles of healing that Jesus does and responses that swirl around him. Tonight I want to tell you about a few subtleties I've noticed.

I think Jesus' keen insight into human nature impresses me as much as anything. For instance, we both attended a banquet not long ago. Jesus noticed that a number of people clamored and scrambled for places at the head table. One guest in particular elbowed his way to the place immediately next to the host's couch. Jesus touched my elbow and told me to watch the host. The host whispered something to the man who had jostled his way to the place of honor. The man immediately covered his face with his right hand. Even at a fair distance I could see the poor fellow's embarrassment. Did he not recognize the speaker for the evening? I felt embarrassed for him when he looked in the direction the host pointed. Then I felt a strange sense of relief that this had not happened to me. I watched the man make his way to his assigned seat, and I wondered what he'd talk about when he found his proper place. I guess it took him a while to gather his wits.

Jesus recalled this incident, without naming names of course because he didn't want to further embarrass anyone when he talked with the disciples later. Sometimes the subtleties reveal as much as highly visible actions. Jesus notices characteristics about human behavior, and this ability attracts me to him. He has an uncanny knack for seeing into the nature of things and drawing insight from matter-of-fact events. He selects illustrations from commonplace occurrences, such as a woman finding a coin, brothers arguing, a father glancing in the direction of his wayward son's departure. Don't misunderstand me. Though he talks about common experiences, not everyone understands him.

Let me give you an illustration. The other day another street character found Jesus. Jesus bought lunch for him. I overheard a man standing near me mutter, "You'd think a rabbi would have better sense than to associate with him." In a moment of genius Jesus raised a question. If ninety-nine out of a herd of one hundred sheep were safely in the pen, wouldn't the shepherd go to find the missing one? The man stood still, looked at Jesus, and muttered, "I am talking about the company you keep and you ask me about how a shepherd acts."

Some people will never understand Jesus, just as some people won't get a joke even if it's explained to them.

Blessings to you,
Eli

Biblical Reflection

Hearing Jesus speak stirs something lost deep inside you. You've not wanted to reveal to anyone how very much alone and lost you sometimes feel. However, when Jesus speaks you want to talk with him. You want to bare your soul to him. Imagine having a half hour alone with Jesus. "Would you really search after me?" you want to ask. Go ahead, pose the question. Tell him that you've always heard that we must seek Jesus. These stories speak of the lost ones being sought after. Ask Jesus if he would seek you out. Watch his eyes as he answers you. Watch his hands as he reaches toward you. He grasps your hands in his. Then he speaks. "Yes," he says, "I mean it when I say that I would look for you." Now, listen as Jesus speaks your name and tells you he is glad he has found you.

Contemporary Reflections

🐟 Imagine yourself in a large room with many tables set for supper. At the far end of the room you see Jesus talking with a few people. You've heard him speak but at a distance. You've seen him but again at a distance. Something about his manner catches your interest, and you find yourself watching him intently. Then he turns toward you, and he catches your eye. You feel modest embarrassment since you had not realized you were staring. Instead of avoiding your glance, Jesus motions for you to come to him. He'd like to have you sit with him at his table. How does he gesture to you? He mouths words, "Come on up here with me." How do the other people with whom he'd been speaking react? Describe their expressions.

🐟 As you approach Jesus, he reaches toward you. What do you imagine him saying to you? What might be the first topic of dinner conversation? What questions does Jesus ask you? What would make you feel comfortable enough to ask him a question?

🐟 Evidence indicates that Jesus enjoyed a good party, a good meal. Imagine yourself sitting at table with Jesus. One of your friends tells a joke. How does Jesus laugh?

Note your reactions as you followed the suggestions for reflection. Describe any comfort, discomfort, or new insights about yourself or about Jesus in your journal. What implications for your life might come from this encounter with scripture?

Day 19

My Good Friend,

It appears to me that Jesus has reached a kind of rhythm
in his ministry. I mentioned Jesus' stories, what I call
his jokes. Over the past couple of days he told two in
particular that still have people muttering. The first has to
do with a father and his two sons. The younger boy
wishes that his father were dead. He takes his part of the
inheritance and goes off on a wild spree. The older son
dutifully remains at home. At last the younger son returns
home, looking quite a bit worse for wear and without a
coin to his name. The father leaps; well, he jumps as high
as an old man can and declares the rest of the day off for a
party. Among the people that I've talked with, none of
them liked the story. Practically everyone did not approve
of the responsible older son's being so shortchanged.
Jesus used humor to sneak up on people. Humor offers a
great way to get at something that might otherwise be
threatening. Of course, people have to get the joke.

Not long after telling that story, Jesus related another
one about a steward who had been caught red-handed
wasting his employer's goods. Realizing that he had
no other marketable skills and that any notion of a
recommendation by his employer was out of the question,
he went to every single client, reduced the debt, and
revised the accounts book. When the employer heard

about the fellow's actions, he commended the man for his shrewd assessment of his circumstances and the astute way of making certain that he had a future.

I'll be honest with you. I like Jesus' stories. I'll tell you this, if Jesus can't do anything else, he can tell a joke! When Jesus tells a story, there's no knowing where it will end up.

Blessings to you,
Eli

Biblical Reflections

🐦 Explanations may leave some people cold. Stories have a way of bringing an idea to life. Imagine hearing Jesus tell each of these stories for the first time. Which character in each story do you immediately like? Which characters do you not like?

🐦 The story of the dishonest steward bothers some people because the man's business ethics are questionable. Yet Jesus tells the story and wishes out loud that his disciples will be at least as smart as the shrewd fellow. In a moment of honesty you may wish that you could tell Jesus exactly what you think of a story containing questionable ethics. What do you tell Jesus?

🐦 Jesus knows that he is telling two stories that will challenge his disciples. What tone of voice do you hear him use? As he concludes each story, watch his eyes. What do you see?

Contemporary Reflection

Assume for a moment that you have been given authority to edit the story of Jesus. Before you take offense at such an idea, remember we are exercising our imaginations. You have found these two stories. During a conversation with friends you have been asked, "Do you intend to keep both stories in the Gospel?" You have a choice to make.

Note your reactions as you followed the suggestions for reflection. Describe any comfort, discomfort, or new insights about yourself or about Jesus in your journal. What implications for your life might come from this encounter with scripture?

Day 20

READ LUKE 14:1-6.

My Good Friend,

Let me tell you what prompts this letter. This notion came
to me after listening to yet another debate between Jesus
and some Pharisees. I hesitate saying this, but at times I
get tired of talking or debating about religion. If I were
to act—care for someone, embrace an enemy, feed the
hungry, behave graciously—that would be closer to
being faithful.

The Pharisees debated again with Jesus about the
sabbath. I don't want to give short shrift to either Jesus
or the Pharisees. On the Pharisees' side rests the great
weight of years of tradition. The sabbath is central in the
Ten Commandments. The prophet Amos railed against
merchants who waited for the sabbath to conclude so
that they could return to the business of making profit. In
exile the captives maintained their identity by keeping the
sabbath. After the return from exile, keeping the sabbath
became a way to include new people in our faith. I can
appreciate why the Pharisees do not tolerate the erosion
of the sabbath.

From Jesus' perspective, the tradition of the sabbath
has become terribly stifling. Following tradition for
tradition's sake puts people at grave risk of losing
conscious purpose. Some Pharisees remember what the
form of religion should look like, but they've lost track of

the content. Perhaps Jesus forces his opponents to rethink what they demand others to do.

I must confess that this discussion itself bores me. As soon as the topic comes up, I want to flee. From my perspective, I'd much rather see something accomplished than to hear yet another debate about policies. As a matter of fact, if I had the courage (or perhaps were foolish enough), I'd say to both Jesus and the Pharisees, "Look, you people have a great deal to offer. Why do you insist on wasting your time talking?" I would remind Jesus of all he has done in Galilee. His reputation has spread far and wide not because of his debating skills. No, his reputation rests on what he does for people: healing, teaching, feeding, and caring. Why has he allowed that great start to bog down in endless discussion? I got so frustrated the other day that I blurted out, "What has this to do with the kingdom of God you keep talking about?"

I hope that discipleship does not include the kind of conversations and debates I have had to endure over the past couple of days. However, I suspect that even disciples may become like Pharisees. Disciples might come to insist on tradition without understanding how closed and rigid they have become. The disciples might equate talking with doing. Lord, have mercy if that happens. The disciples may someday forget that self-righteousness endangers the faith in all times, not just in our time.

Yours,
Eli

Biblical Reflection

Imagine sitting at a table with Jesus and several followers. You and another follower debate what can or cannot be done on the sabbath. He's been in this sort of discussion many times. You become increasingly frustrated. You drum the table with your fingers. Your heart beats faster as you draw your breath to challenge Jesus. "Is this what you had in mind when you called us to discipleship?" What is Jesus' response? What does Jesus yearn to say to you? An uncomfortable silence descends over the group. Everyone in the group is looking first at you then to Jesus. What will he say? You had run out of patience. You became frustrated, feeling Jesus was missing the mark, and you finally challenged him. What does he look like now? Look at his hands. How does he sit at the table? Picture him leaning forward from the edge of his chair. Finally Jesus speaks. Imagine listening intently as he lowers his voice and whispers, "No, what I have always had in mind is . . ." What does he say?

Contemporary Reflection

You and Jesus have arrived at your church for one of the usual monthly committee meetings. You have given Jesus a copy of the agenda to read so that he can participate in the discussion. On the way to the church, he notices something that he wants to suggest as a more important task than the agenda at hand. He has indicated to you that he will ask to speak before the group starts on the agenda. What did Jesus notice? What does he consider more pressing than agenda items? What does he want to say to the group? How do you feel as you antici- pate the committee's response to his challenge? How do you handle the anger of the chair, who insists that a great deal of time and effort has been put into preparing for this meeting? How do you explain that the group's response comes very close to the Pharisees' insistence that Jesus pay attention to their agenda?

Note your reactions as you followed the suggestions for reflection. Describe any comfort, discomfort, or new insights about yourself or about Jesus in your journal. What implications for your life might come from this encounter with scripture?

Day 21

❧ READ LUKE 14:12-14.

My Dear Friend,

Today Jesus talked about dinner parties and the invitation list. He said that when we throw a dinner party, we should invite people who wouldn't stand a chance of being on anyone else's invitation list. He insists that we invite people who couldn't possibly pay us back. Invite the tradesman whose hourly wage barely allows for a home, food, and his children's necessities. Invite the leatherworker who has to stay at work until nearly midnight every day in order to catch up on his backlog of repairs. Invite the two town characters who manage to show up for a banquet but who never seem to have any contribution to make. Invite the street folk who push their carts filled with broken items.

Just for a moment I allowed myself to imagine a dinner party hosted by Jesus: There would be blind people with their guides, crippled people trying not to trip over canes, street people dressed in rags and sandals held together with string. I hope you'll understand when I tell you I burst into laughter and then found myself crying. If the truth were known, I think Jesus' party would include more real humanity, more authentic humanity certainly than the folk I would meet at an elegant gathering. Those street people are lucky to have anyone talk to them, and here Jesus offers the possibility of a real party!

My good friend, I confess that part of me wants to believe what Jesus says. The longer I listen to him, the more I like the kind of life to which he points. Also a part of me wishes I could live a life exclusively with the rich and famous. Why not? Don't we all yearn for what money can buy? If I had the courage, I would ask Jesus if he honestly believes all that he says. If I were to do what Jesus instructs, then I would be hoping that God sees and notes what I do. Why? Because my friends will think I'm crazy! Please keep this to yourself. I don't want anyone else privy to these thoughts.

Perhaps courage will come tomorrow.

Blessings to you,
Eli

Biblical Reflection

Place yourself alongside Jesus as his guests arrive for the meal. Imagine their expressions. They've never been invited anywhere before, much less to a party. Listen to them say, "Thank you." Watch them as they reach toward Jesus to shake his hand.

Contemporary Reflection

Jesus arrives at your home and suggests throwing a party. "Let's invite some folks in for supper," he says. "Let's invite people who wouldn't receive an invitation if they were the last people on earth." The idea sounds good to you. Whom will you invite?

Now you are sitting with Jesus and a street person whom you invited to the party. Jesus wants to say grace before the meal. He reaches out with both hands to you and your guest. The three of you hold hands as Jesus says grace. How do you feel as he holds hands with one of the poor street people who has come to his table? Jesus gives thanks for the day's food, then asks, "What are you giving thanks for today?" What does your guest say to Jesus? What do you tell Jesus?

Note your reactions as you followed the suggestions for reflection. Describe any comfort, discomfort, or new insights about yourself or about Jesus in your journal. What implications for your life might come from this encounter with scripture?

Day 22

🐦 READ LUKE 14:26-35.

My Good Friend,

This letter may have a different tone to it. As time goes on, I dare not confide my private thoughts to anyone but you. Today Jesus said something that bothers me. I shall quote as accurately as I can. "Whoever comes to me and does not hate father and mother, wife and children, brothers and sisters, yes, and even life itself, cannot be my disciple." He went on to give illustrations of what it looks like when people begin major undertakings but cannot finish them. You can say what you will and try to convince me otherwise, but what he said today goes too far. I talked with another man about this. He was hopping mad. How can anyone be willing to give up family?

Yes, I understand the Torah portion that was read during this week's worship concerns precisely this topic of radical obedience. In case you've forgotten, the passage was from Genesis. The reasoning had to do with Abraham's binding of Isaac on Mount Moriah. You'll recall the story. Abraham takes his son to the mountain apparently to perform a ritual sacrifice. At the last critical moment, an angel speaks, and a ram appears—certainly one of the most compelling and dramatic incidents in all of scripture. The man with whom I spoke declared that if this kind of demand defines religion, he doesn't want any part of it. Jesus and anyone else could count him out!

According to Jesus, we must be willing to forsake our family. Granted, times come when parents and children don't want to see each other. I've known those times and so have you. Those moments reflect more or less part of the natural course of being a family. Jesus talks, however, about not necessarily a normal course of events.

These kinds of radical demands in the name of religion always disturb me. I don't mind giving a little of myself. I don't mind being a little different from other people. However, my discomfort with living in a way that separates me from family and friends hinders my response to Jesus. In recent days I think and feel much more strongly as if I want to follow Jesus. I have felt myself increasingly embrace Jesus' teaching and want very much to respond to his invitation to discipleship. But when Jesus makes absolute demands, I have to confess— in my prayers if nowhere else—that I honestly hesitate to follow Jesus. This part of Jesus' teaching doesn't make sense to me.

I shall write more later. For now, this will be enough. I am confused.

Blessings,
Eli

Biblical Reflections

❧ You dare not utter some of your feelings about discipleship, even in your prayers. Imagine hearing Jesus issue this radical summons to discipleship. How do you feel as you hear him? Everything in you wants to ask for clarifications. Is he serious about these stringent demands? You summon the courage to ask your question. Jesus pauses momentarily and then responds. What does Jesus say? How does his face look as he answers your question?

➤ You try to tell Jesus that you want to be a disciple, and you will work at it. What emotions do you feel as you attempt to tell him that you want to be a disciple while at the same time you feel yourself fudging a bit?

Contemporary Reflection

You have met Jesus for lunch and sit down at a booth in a restaurant. He wants to have that conversation you mentioned, the one about being a disciple. You tell him about your own situation in life and the challenges to being a disciple. He takes your questions seriously and asks for your thoughts. He asks you, "What conditions would you suggest for discipleship?" What do you want to tell him? How does he respond? What stories from your life would you include as illustrations?

Note your reactions as you followed the suggestions for reflection. Describe any comfort, discomfort, or new insights about yourself or about Jesus in your journal. What implications for your life might come from this encounter with scripture?

Fourth Sunday in Lent

LUKE 14:15-26

My Dear Friend,

I want to talk with you about something to which I have alluded in earlier correspondence. Put quite bluntly, if we take Jesus seriously, we risk looking very foolish. Bear with me as I work through these thoughts.

Jesus visits with people I usually would not want to encounter even in passing. Here's what surprises me: Now I want to visit with these people as well as more acceptable people. I told a friend the other day that I find more authenticity in common folk than I ever thought possible. In fact, I find the poor folk more open than many wealthy people I know. Although I did notice a change in some wealthier folk who ate supper with Jesus recently. They dropped their defenses and pretensions and became much more human. They talked about the common stuff of life and the basics of getting by. Jesus has a way of getting through to the inner person. You might want to ask, "What has this to do with looking foolish?" My answer is simple. If I declared that people are people and money makes no difference, social standing makes no difference, success or failure makes no difference, people may think that I have lost my mind. They may wish to protest, saying that in fact those things do make a difference. Well, they don't to Jesus! And increasingly they are not making much difference to me.

Besides looking foolish, a second range of consequences when I take Jesus seriously is a change in how I regard details of everyday life. Jesus sees in the incidents of everyday life lessons and stories with moral content and ethical imperative. No one I've met before possesses this uncanny ability; nor can anyone else carry it off with such facility. If I tried this kind of interpretation, I would sound overbearing or ridiculously simplistic. Of course some people think that Jesus comes on too strong and that his stories don't make any sense. Some resent his constant challenges; however, his insights into human nature and his keen observations of people always impress me. As you know, I hold in very high esteem anyone with the capacity of moral issues at stake in any circumstance. I wish I had that ability myself. Perhaps that's part of why I like to be around Jesus. He sees more than I see and can draw out implications.

I have one further thought I want to tell you. Jesus speaks unabashedly about what he calls the kingdom of God. He constantly points out that life is different in the kingdom of God. I get the distinct impression that he speaks not about a time in an indistinct future. He sounds as if he understands the kingdom as going on right now, right here, in his presence, with people he meets and in the actions he performs. He acts and speaks as if the kingdom is present. I appreciate the fact that what he creates around him differs from what I see around other people. He is more sensitive to all people than anyone I've met. He acts out of a different set of priorities, a different orientation toward life's purpose.

My major anxiety now is that if I live as Jesus invites me to live, as if he speaks truth and envisions both reality and possibility, then I shall differ from people around me.

My own way of thinking and living will change. I already feel changes taking place in both my thinking and my actions. I remain reluctant to join him wholeheartedly. Nevertheless, do you remember how I looked at Jesus from a distance in Galilee? I feel myself drawn closer to him now. I no longer want to stand at the edge of the crowd all the time. I want to be closer.

Blessings,
Eli

Biblical Reflections

❧ Today Jesus suggests that you go for a long walk together. Your walk begins near the center of town. As you walk toward the town's boundary and the desert beyond, Jesus stops momentarily to point out something. What does he see that warrants his attention? What part of nature appeals to him today? If he sees a person, who is it? Describe what Jesus points out to you.

❧ Spend some time walking with Jesus. How do the stones feel under your feet? As you walk with Jesus, notice his stride. Note how he swings his arms. Listen to him whistle. How do you feel?

❧ You have been walking for the better part of an hour. You've been thinking about what you have seen in Galilee, what Jesus has preached about on the way to Jerusalem, and now you want to tell him something. You want to point out one characteristic in him that you find most interesting, intriguing, or inviting. What will you tell him?

Contemporary Reflection

Imagine Jesus being active in your community right now. You've spent a lot of time listening and watching him. He has worked miracles and touched people in remarkable ways. One of your friends is suffering (perhaps from self-doubt, a painful memory, or depression about work). This friend asks you to introduce him or her to Jesus. You arrange a meeting in your town's park. As you come together, you say, "Jesus, I would like you to meet my good friend. . . ." What characteristic would you want to mention in your introduction? Then you introduce Jesus to your friend, saying, "[Name], I would like you to meet Jesus." What characteristic about Jesus do you include in your introduction?

Note your reactions as you followed the suggestions for reflection. Describe any comfort, discomfort, or new insights about yourself or about Jesus in your journal. What implications for your life might come from this encounter with scripture?

Day 23

My Good Friend,

Not many people overheard the conversation I'm going to tell you about today. I did and must share it with you. One of Jesus' followers grew impatient. From what I could gather, the man had been working pretty hard recently, hadn't had much time to himself, and was worn out and tired. When he told Jesus his story, Jesus didn't say much in reply.

Clearly the man wanted Jesus to notice his efforts, how hard he'd been working and how much time he'd spent on the job. Jesus wouldn't take any of his prompts. He responded to none of the man's cajoling. Finally Jesus said that a follower cannot expect compliments for doing what should be done. You don't get compliments for doing what should have been done in the first place.

Jesus will have nothing to do with sentimentalized religion. Plenty of work remains to be done; there are people to see, study to pursue, and livelihoods to be earned. If people are looking for a messiah who will congratulate them for every detail of their work, then they should start looking someplace else because Jesus simply will not embody that kind of messiah. Granted, we all want our efforts acknowledged. I desire Jesus' acknowledgment as much as anyone else. However, Jesus particularly intends to secure disciples who care about the work more than they care about getting credit for doing the work.

Though I take offense occasionally, I still appreciate the stringent demands Jesus makes. Thus, for the time being, I will close since I should complete the work assigned to me today. I have been asked to visit some people who wanted to see Jesus but were too sick to leave their homes. Jesus told me to take his blessing to them. When evening comes, I hope to be satisfied that I have done my duty, have done my work well, and have lived faithfully. That will be enough.

Blessings to you,

Elí

Biblical Reflections

🌱 Imagine spending an hour with Jesus as he travels from one town to the next. Earlier in the day he told you that he would like to hear about your work, your work as a disciple. How did he ask you? What do you want to tell him about your work? How does following Jesus affect you in your work?

🌱 Though Jesus has admonished disciples not to seek praise, you yearn to hear Jesus' acknowledgment for something you have done. What accomplishment would you like to tell Jesus about? For his part, even though he told disciples not to seek praise, Jesus makes a gesture and says a brief word to you. Name that gesture. Name that word.

Contemporary Reflection

Jesus visits your church, and you have an opportunity to speak with him. You are concerned about someone who needs to hear an encouraging word. She or he has been ignored and over-looked for too long. You ask Jesus to speak to that person; he accedes to your request and asks you to arrange the meeting. Afterward Jesus speaks to you about how you might continue to encourage this person when he is gone. What suggestions does he make?

Note your reactions as you followed the suggestions for reflection. Describe any comfort, discomfort, or new insights about yourself or about Jesus in your journal. What implications for your life might come from this encounter with scripture?

Day 24

🪱 READ LUKE 18:9-14.

My Good Friend,

I've told you about Jesus' stories. He caught me in one of those stories today. He told of two men who go to the Temple to pray: the first one, a high-profile member of the congregation, well known for his substantial contributions and status in the community; the other, known only as "Boots," found regularly drinking out of a wineskin in the marketplace. It seems that the first man's prayers included reference to his duties (always well performed), his contributions (always up-to-date), and the fact that he differed from the other man. The second man appeared uncomfortable in the sanctuary. Say what you will about the house of the Lord being open to all, we all know that some people look rather peculiar in those ornate surroundings. "Boots" didn't even look up. He only muttered something about his sins. Then he left.

As Jesus concluded the story, I whispered to the woman standing next to me, "I'm glad I differ from that rich fellow; I might have been a target for Jesus' joke this time." Jesus must have heard me because he glanced in my direction. Something about the look in his eye and the way he raised his eyebrow told me I had been like that rich fellow! I'd been caught in the joke!

You don't have any idea how much I'd like to launch into a description of what I've learned or how this might apply to other people. That, however, would only blunt the embarrassment I feel about having fallen into the trap of thinking myself better than someone else.

In previous letters I've told you how Jesus notes and talks about subtleties of life that I see in my own experience. I doubt that I will ever seize the opportunity to heal or preach as Jesus does or the disciples do. But I can do the little things, acts that often are overlooked but make a disproportionate amount of difference. When I think of how important these small gestures are and about how often I miss the mark, I doubt I'll think arrogantly of myself again. In this manner, I hope to be faithful with a little or a lot.

Blessings to you,

Eli

Biblical Reflections

🥐 Sooner or later we will find ourselves the object of one of Jesus' lessons. Embarrassment may follow. Think of a story Jesus tells that makes you uncomfortable. Imagine hearing the story for the first time in his presence. You become caught up in the story and then recognize yourself in it. What embarrasses you? How do you react—in word or gesture?

🥐 Imagine yourself as the one in the sanctuary who cannot lift your eyes to look at heaven. You see the wealthy man at a distance and avoid his glance. Then you realize that someone stands with you. Jesus stands with you. He whispers, "I know what's on your mind. I know what troubles you." He continues whispering to you, saying that he prays for you. What do you say to Jesus as he concludes his prayer for you?

Contemporary Reflection

In your heart of hearts perhaps you harbor the notion (or the hope?) that the Lord hears prayers from certain people more readily than the prayers of others. Imagine standing in a sanctuary with someone you do not like or you have considered different or below you in status. Jesus stands next to you. He wants to tell you what he notices about the other person. What does Jesus see? How does he tell you about his observation and insight? You want to know how to pray for the other person. He offers to say a prayer for him or her. Listen to Jesus as he prays on behalf of the one whom you expected God to ignore until your concerns had been tended to.

Note your reactions as you followed the suggestions for reflection. Describe any comfort, discomfort, or new insights about yourself or about Jesus in your journal. What implications for your life might come from this encounter with scripture?

Day 25

READ LUKE 17:20-37.

My Good Friend,

You may have recovered from the shock you felt when I characterized Jesus' stories as jokes. The more I think of it, the more I believe the characterization's accuracy. In a conversation I overheard, Jesus said as much. Let me tell you about it.

Recently some Pharisees asked Jesus when the kingdom of God would come. The question is on everyone's mind these days. Lots of people look for a time when history finally will bend in favor of justice and the common good, and Judea will be free of an occupation army. As you know, a number of individuals attempt to bring the kingdom by force. They have all been crushed ruthlessly. For other people, the kingdom seems a bit unrealistic, almost ethereal. They seem to have given up altogether. They live as if there is no tomorrow worth waiting for. The question lingers: When will the kingdom of God come? When this whole drama called history will reach its climax interests me too. I listened to Jesus keenly.

From what I can gather, according to Jesus, all sorts of fanfare or other discernible signs will not usher in the kingdom. *Oh boy,* I thought, *that will surprise and bother people who look forward to clouds parting, trumpets blaring, and a celestial display erupting.* But if the kingdom won't come in like that, how will it come?

I hope that I am not misquoting Jesus. I thought I heard him say that the kingdom of God is "among you." I felt a bit light-headed when I heard him say that. Did he mean to suggest that he brings the kingdom? Surely that exaggerates too much. Did he mean to suggest that any proper notion of the kingdom must be seen and lived in the everyday common stuff of life? I've mentioned any number of times that Jesus points to everyday things. His stories include objects and events like lost coins, lost sheep, a son angrily slamming a door, and a military commander carefully considering the odds of victory in an upcoming campaign. Jesus seems to say that ordinary daily occurrences make up the kingdom. Do you suppose that the kingdom of God, elaborate and exciting as it sounds, might also consist of the normal activities of life lived in different, imaginative ways?

Somehow the kingdom of God exists within the capacity of people to achieve. At this point I confess that God has more confidence in people than I do. Frankly, I doubt that the kingdom of God will be achieved this side of judgment. I just don't see it happening within history. I don't have sufficient confidence in the abilities of people to do what it would take, to give up what would have to be given up, to concede to the common good, to give up privileges of a few . . . my list goes on too long.

Having said all this, however, I must say that the notion of the kingdom being "within" us challenges me. I cannot close until I share one more thought. I wrote this letter a few days ago and hesitated to send it. I prefer to cling to the hope of God's confidence in us rather than concede to despair. Spending this time with Jesus changes me. I witness Jesus' influence, and I want to believe that the kingdom can come. I prefer a world in which the kingdom is imaginable to a world in which it is unimaginable.

Blessings,

Eli

Biblical Reflections

❧ Imagine Jesus coming to you in the middle of the morning. The previous day he'd seen you at the gathering where he talked about the kingdom of God in the midst of us. He asks, "What comes to your mind when you hear me speak of the kingdom?" What image comes to your mind? What event or people do you describe to him?

❧ Eli reports a growing awareness of God's confidence in people. Imagine sitting with Jesus. You want to ask him a question. You know yourself well enough to wonder how Jesus could have confidence in you. You wish that you could confess this self-awareness to Jesus. "Jesus," you say, "you speak of the kingdom among us. There's something about me that you need to know, something that I suspect interferes with the kingdom present in me." What do you want to confess to Jesus? How does he receive your confession? Imagine now that you've confessed, said the unmentionable things that impede the kingdom. Now listen to Jesus' assurance. What does he say? What is his tone? Now imagine Jesus putting his arm around your shoulder. Listen as he says, "The kingdom is within you."

Contemporary Reflection

While out on some errands you noticed a particularly poignant scene. You observed someone acting in a way that prompted you to think, *That's what the kingdom of God among us means.* Describe what you saw. Perhaps a person acted in a particularly gracious and unassuming manner or risked criticism for supporting a marginal person in the community. What made you think of the presence of the kingdom in that person's actions? Now imagine describing the scene to Jesus. You want to make certain you understood what he said. How does Jesus receive your description? What does Jesus have to say about your sensitivity to and perception of the kingdom of God among us?

Note your reactions as you followed the suggestions for reflection. Describe any comfort, discomfort, or new insights about yourself or about Jesus in your journal. What implications for your life might come from this encounter with scripture?

Day 26

My Good Friend,

This morning Jesus told a really good one, one of the best tales I've heard. Someone asked him how we should pray, so Jesus told a story about a judge and a widow.

The judge was known to be a hardnose who showed little compassion for anyone. The proficient judge graduated first in his class, but he cared not so much about the law as he did about fees he could charge. Small wonder then that when a poor woman tried to get a hearing in his court, he had no time for her. Try as she might, she could not get past his court clerk. That poor woman badgered the judge's clerk for weeks.

Finally the clerk began to relent. He couldn't take the constant petitioning anymore and decided to risk his boss's censure. Approaching the judge, he whispered, "Sir, could you please see . . ." I'd like to have heard the judge's answer. Even the most hardened men have their limits. The judge relented because he and the clerk were so annoyed by the woman's badgering. He'd said to himself once too often, *Though I care little about anyone or God, I simply cannot afford to lose more time.* The court clerk could hardly get any work done either.

I suspect that if this story is told in the future, a laugh may sweep through the crowd. It creates a comical picture—a widow in threadbare clothes entering the inner sanctum of a mighty judge and getting—by sheer dint of her persistence—the best service the man can offer. Ethics notwithstanding, the story illustrates the urgency and intensity of prayer. Remember that the disciples had asked Jesus how we should pray. He tells of a desperate woman who risks everything and leaves no effort untapped in order to get what she needs. The woman makes me feel embarrassed and uncomfortable for two reasons. Her untoward and unguarded actions draw too much attention to herself. I remember times when I too acted presumptuously or in a forward way.

More importantly, however, and far more tellingly, I have not prayed with that kind of intensity. I simply haven't prayed as I should. Until recently nothing has seemed to warrant urgent and single-minded prayer. I feel guilty that I have waited until I desperately needed God's help before I started praying intensely. Until now my most authentic prayer would have been thanksgiving not to be in circumstances as desperate as that widow's. In more recent days, Jesus' words mean more to me. I want to understand him. His insight and wisdom feel really promising. I am praying. Please pray for me.

Blessings to you,

Eli

Biblical Reflections

✤ Picture yourself among that group of people who hear Jesus tell this story. Though you've managed to keep your innermost concerns to yourself, Jesus' urgency causes you momentarily to drop your guard. Those concerns rush to the surface.

You'd like to tell Jesus what troubles your soul nearly to desperation. Your heart pounds, your breath quickens, and you want to tell Jesus your desire for prayer. In fact, you want Jesus to pray with you. For what personal issue do you want Jesus to pray?

✎ Jesus' manner in telling the story suggests he would be willing to hear you confess that you haven't believed in prayer. You don't want to tell him. But if you're to be honest with Jesus, you have to tell him not only the shining moments of faith but the moments of doubt as well. Jesus senses your discomfort as you attempt to fashion a few words. How does he listen? Relax as Jesus reaches toward you reassuringly.

Contemporary Reflection

Jesus surprises you with his request: He wants you to pray for him. He surprises you even more by asking you to pray for a part of his ministry particularly important to you. What part of Jesus' ministry especially touches your heart? What do you pray? Write your prayer.

Note your reactions as you followed the suggestions for reflection. Describe any comfort, discomfort, or new insights about yourself or about Jesus in your journal. What implications for your life might come from this encounter with scripture?

Day 27

רא*? READ LUKE 18:35-43.

My Good Friend,

What I saw today makes me want to write and write a lot.
Everything is getting more intense as we get closer to
Jerusalem. The tensions that build around Jesus feel
almost unbearably high. My emotions run at a fever pitch
today. Incredibly, as the tension increases, Jesus still pays
attention to people.

As we approached Jericho, a blind man startled us all
when he shouted out, "Jesus, Son of David, have mercy
on me!" Once again I felt quite uncomfortable. The man's
contorted face revealed encrusted eyes. All the rest of us
did not know what to do. But Jesus stopped and walked
over to the poor fellow. He asked what the man wanted
him to do. At first blush it seemed patently obvious what
the man needed. He wanted to be able to see. Why then
would Jesus ask what appears an unnecessary question—
in fact, a silly question? I wanted to say, "Jesus, did you
see the man's eyes? What else would he rather have you
do?" But I didn't. Besides, I am not comfortable enough
with Jesus to challenge him in public. Still, it seemed a
foolish question. If I had asked the blind man the same
question, I would not have been able to provide the help
he required. When Jesus asked the open-ended question,
he implied that he could do whatever the man asked
him to do. I suppose that by asking the question, Jesus

required the blind man to assume some responsibility for his own healing.

When Jesus pays attention to people, listens carefully, and then heals, I am still stunned, amazed, and shocked. I expected Jesus to touch the man, to rub his eyes, to do something. Instead he simply spoke, "Receive your sight; your faith has saved you." Everyone with me was shocked. The man focused for the first time in years. He erupted into uncontrollable joy. I cried along with him. You know, as many times as I have seen Jesus accomplish a healing, it never fails to touch me deeply when I see a life changed so dramatically. It didn't surprise me in the least that the man immediately joined the disciples and followed Jesus.

I can only imagine having sight restored. Jesus said that the man's faith had restored his sight. If Jesus were to ask what I would like him to do for me, I'd make this request: I would like to have sufficient faith for him to say, "Your faith has saved you." I've been with Jesus quite a while now. I've watched him and listened to him. What he does and says always touches and moves me, but I'm still hesitant about joining him wholeheartedly. However, seeing what can happen when he encounters a person with faith not only amazes me but stirs a desire for a similar faith. You'll never know how much I wish for faith like that of the Roman centurion in Capernaum, the woman who elbowed her way through the crowd, the friends who brought the crippled man to Jesus, and now this blind man. Jesus said those marvelous words, "Faith has healed you." I can't imagine how good that would feel to have Jesus acknowledge my faith.

I hope this doesn't sound too far-fetched, but I wonder if perhaps this miracle of restoring sight isn't also about how a person looks at life. I suspect more was going on than just restoring sight. Certainly since I've been listening to Jesus, I look at life differently. Remember how he said the kingdom of God is within you? I look for moments when I see that kingdom. I still ponder his stories. His insights always stimulate me. Frankly, I've wondered if perhaps even people with perfect eyesight could benefit from Jesus' healing words.

When the man declared his wish to become a disciple, Jesus didn't prohibit him. Do you remember the incident in the graveyard in Gerasenes? Jesus wouldn't let that man follow him. This time Jesus allows the healed man to follow. Do you suppose Jesus feels more anxious as he gets closer to Jerusalem? Does Jesus realize that he will need more followers? Will it surprise you if I tell you that I am becoming more of a follower? For reasons not entirely clear to me, I find myself thinking increasingly of the truth of what Jesus says and does. Like the healed man, I too want to follow Jesus. It has taken this long for me to arrive at this point. As I said earlier, tensions have built. Do you suppose some people are drawn to Jesus precisely at times of stress?

Blessings to you,

Elí

Biblical Reflections

☙ You overhear Jesus speaking to the blind man. The question "What do you want me to do for you?" sounds almost too good to be true. The man can ask for anything. He asks for restored sight. As you witness this healing, you find yourself moving away to a quiet place where no one can see you. You've allowed the same question to get into your own soul and you find yourself saying, "Jesus, if you could only know my need deep in my soul." What do you want to ask Jesus to heal?

❧ Eli appears to draw closer to Jesus. He notices how many times Jesus points to people's faith as central to their healing. Allow yourself an imaginary conversation with this formerly blind man. Since he has decided to follow Jesus, you and he are able to walk together for quite some distance. What feelings do you have as you hear him talk about his faith? What does he say to you about faith? How did he hear about Jesus?

Contemporary Reflection

Disfigurement, blindness, abnormality often threaten us. Do you feel uncomfortable when you see people who are afflicted in some way? Imagine walking with Jesus along a street in your community or city. You reach an intersection where a blind man or woman stands. Other people are standing there too, but Jesus seems not to see them. He focuses on the blind person. He then tells you what he sees when he looks at a person or hears a person request help. What does Jesus see in street people? What does Jesus note when he sees a blind woman? What does Jesus point out to you? What do you say to Jesus as you recognize your common humanity with Jesus and the ignored street person?

Note your reactions as you followed the suggestions for reflection. Describe any comfort, discomfort, or new insights about yourself or about Jesus in your journal. What implications for your life might come from this encounter with scripture?

Day 28

❧ READ LUKE 19:41-44.

My Good Friend,

Jesus finally reached his destination. We have arrived in
Jerusalem. The mood here differs considerably from that
in the north country. The glad days of miracles, preaching,
and long walks in Galilee are gone now. I didn't realize
how different it would be here until we entered the city.
When we cleared the brow of the hill, Jesus burst into
tears. I thought initially that his tears might have been the
result of pent-up emotion from a long-awaited pilgrimage.
That happened to me when I saw my family's graves for
the first time. I also felt like this when I finally saw the old
farmhouse in which I spent my first eight years. Jesus cried
when he saw the city skyline.

After composing himself, Jesus whispered his deep
desire for people to pursue actions that foster peace. This
saddened me as well. The undercurrent of seething anger
runs strong throughout the territory—and especially in
the city. Jesus knows the inevitable result if an uprising
erupts. Roman legions can inflict terrific suffering and
destruction. The dreadful consequences of Jerusalem's fall
centuries ago will pale in comparison. Jesus can see over
the horizon. He carries a peculiar burden, as does anyone
who can see the consequences of today's actions long
before others consider the possibilities.

Jesus shows enormous compassion. Perhaps his tears

result from contained anguish over what people endure. He has seen all kinds of people and cared for innumerable needs. Surely Jesus bears within his own soul a deep concern for people. Small wonder then, with all he has done, all he has encountered, all the caring he's offered people, and all he can see, that he broke down in tears.

How awfully unfair that he weeps for people even as some of those people already have turned against him. When I recall the care that Jesus has poured out and then see people who want to argue about what he can and cannot do on a sabbath, I want to cry too. Some other people seem always ready to pick a fight over traditions Jesus appears to ignore. Others pick at him because he speaks in riddles. It doesn't surprise me at all that the man breaks down in tears. Even though he has poured out his soul for people, he receives only an argument or rejection. He has tried to do his best for them. Even his gift of healing has been misunderstood and misinterpreted. Nevertheless he persevered. Jesus sat with the disconsolate, wept with the grief-stricken, held the hands of a sobbing mother, sat silently as a father wept for his wayward son, and prayed with a dying friend. I've told you about some spectacular events. But Jesus avoided always working in a public way. I guess that for every one of his public actions there must have been a lot of things he did in private where only he and one other person would know what transpired. Then, after all that, to have people turn against him. I am crying now.

I said earlier that Jesus hasn't time for sentimentality in religion. The tears he wept upon entering Jerusalem were hardly the stuff of sentimentality. The tears that I saw today came from deep within his soul. I hope he's up to what this city will demand of him. Certainly events have begun to take on a life of their own and a volatility that I've not seen previously. For Jesus and all who follow him, these next few days will be very difficult. Please pray for Jesus and pray for all of his followers. Since I am becoming a follower, I will ask you to pray for me as well.

Blessings to you,

Eli

Biblical Reflections

❧ Jesus has cared for people in all sorts of ways. He has touched the crippled, spoken to the forgotten, eaten meals with outcasts, and spent time with deeply troubled people. All were touched deeply. Some other people insist on arguing and starting a fight. Imagine sitting with Jesus at the end of the day on which he entered Jerusalem. The day has been long. You and Jesus both notice your weariness. Yet you cannot comfortably let the day conclude without asking Jesus about his tears and his concern for peace. You want to ask Jesus what makes him weep. Then you want to ask him what people should know in order to pursue peace. He turns the question on you. "Have you ever cried at the terrible possibilities that may befall people?" he asks. He waits for your response.

❧ Jesus then reflects back your second question. He asks, "What do you think makes for peace?" You know that in answering the question you must include something about your resistance to doing what you know Jesus expects. How will you answer him?

Contemporary Reflection

For a moment allow yourself to look at your city, your town, your church as Jesus might. He sees what others haven't seen. He feels deeply what others may not yet have begun to feel. You hear him say, ever so softly, "Would that you knew the things that make for peace." What does Jesus see? What stirs his soul to the point of crying?

Note your reactions as you followed the suggestions for reflection. Describe any comfort, discomfort, or new insights about yourself or about Jesus in your journal. What implications for your life might come from this encounter with scripture?

Fifth Sunday in Lent

❧ READ LUKE 19:28-32.

My Dear Friend,

Today Jesus instructed his disciples to prepare a seder meal. Evidently Jesus intends to ride back into Jerusalem. The instructions included a bit about contacting a man who owns a colt. Someone assisted Jesus by providing the animal anonymously.

Recall the stories of Elijah. One in particular came to mind today. Elijah had run as fast as he could from the charred embers and bleeding corpses on Mount Carmel. Scared to within an inch of his life, he hid in a cave. When he talked with the Lord again, he presented his case for "prophet of the year" award. He went so far as to assert that he was the only one in all Israel who worked hard for the purposes of the Lord. Finally the Lord grew impatient with the prophet's self-promotion and reminded him that seven thousand others had not yet succumbed to the demands of the state. A friend of mine calls this attitude the "Elijah syndrome."

Why did I think of that story? Many people work in obscure, anonymous ways. Their work equals that of the well-known personalities in the grand scheme of things. The name of that man providing the colt Jesus will ride into Jerusalem will forever be unknown. Nevertheless he prepared to supply necessary transportation. His act, a courageous action, defied the city filled with spies.

Military forces constantly monitored all activities. The people who prepared the seder meal for Jesus and his disciples exhibited courage. Even though they provided a crucial service, their names may be forever lost.

You may wonder why these preparations affect me as they do. On my good days I want to believe that the Lord knows the efforts of both the famous and the obscure. On my bad days I want almost desperately to be named, to be known, to leave a mark on the record of history. Then I look at the numbers. Elijah was but one name in all Israel. The Lord reminded him that fully seven thousand remained unnamed, obscure, anonymous. I know of twelve named disciples. We could assume that for each one of them, thousands more people quietly and unobtrusively work for Jesus' purposes. For today I shall take this calculation as confirmation that the Lord has many on Jesus' side.

Every blessing to you,

Eli

Biblical Reflections

☙ Picture yourself talking with the unnamed man whose animal Jesus has requested for transportation into Jerusalem. How did he hear about Jesus? How were the arrangements made for the animal to be available? Who contacted him? What assurances did he receive? What prompted him to collaborate with Jesus' movement?

☙ Imagine the disciples hearing someone talk about the man who provided the animal. He isn't named, but the disciples may have known him. Imagine one of the disciples saying,

"I wish that one action I took could be remembered." Imagine one action, one moment, in which a disciple might have assisted Jesus. Describe that moment.

Contemporary Reflection

One reading of Jesus' entry into Jerusalem suggests Roman officials viewed the Jesus movement as a clandestine organization intent on revolt against the empire. How do you feel being a part of a movement that may be misunderstood? Reflect on stories from history about underground movements such as the Underground Railroad or heroic citizens like Corrie ten Boom who hid Jews from the Nazis during World War II. What prompts people to participate in underground movements? Imagine being asked to participate in the Jesus movement. You run grave risk of punishment if you are caught or implicated by others who have been caught. How do you respond?

Note your reactions as you followed the suggestions for reflection. Describe any comfort, discomfort, or new insights about yourself or about Jesus in your journal. What implications for your life might come from this encounter with scripture?

Day 29

My Good Friend,

Most of the people I visited today want to talk about the way Jesus entered Jerusalem. A story Jesus told before he entered the city still intrigues me. The story told about a wealthy man who, prior to departing for a long business trip, distributed investment capital among a number of his subordinates. When he returned, he demanded an accounting of and return on those investments. Most of the subordinates reported interest earned. The financier awarded each of them more money, a larger responsibility. One man, however, chose not to invest. Fearful that if he failed, the financier would be angry with him and penalize him, he hid his money. What if his investment had lost value? Surely the financier would have been upset, so this man chose not to invest in what could prove a disaster. What appeared to be prudence turned out to be ill-advised. The financier took away everything he had given to this man.

I don't like these challenges that lead to failure. The more I thought of that story, the more upset I became. Does Jesus mean to suggest that he expects us to take risks on his behalf, on behalf of what he calls the kingdom of God? As a matter of fact, Jesus has employed these "lose your life and save it" motifs along the way. Some of Jesus' followers argued about what this story meant. A few of the frustrated followers finally declared their wish that Jesus would say what he means instead of constantly telling these stories. Granted, some of the followers enjoy the stories and the process of interpreting the ambiguities. They claim to employ their imaginations more when Jesus tells a story than when he states a teaching unequivocally. One fellow I know summoned up his courage and asked, pointedly, why in the midst of life-and-death issues any leader would speak in riddles and stories. What happens if followers misunderstand or misinterpret what Jesus says? The catastrophic result could parallel an army's misunderstanding the commanding officer's orders. The same fellow protested that he himself would have issued clear instructions with no chance of misunderstanding.

Rather than debate Jesus' manner, I will point to one fact. When Jesus speaks of challenges authentically risky, he matches his words with his actions. When he issues challenges to people, he also issues them to himself. I admit that a story of risk sounds a great deal more authentic here in Jerusalem than in the safe environs of Galilee. If Jesus had remained in Galilee, this story of risk taking would not sound as strong as it did today. His risk taking lends authority to his story.

In Jerusalem, under the shadow of Roman military rule, tensions run high. Even innocent people suffer under Roman oppression. In the midst of all this, Jesus hazards his own life. No one can accuse him of demanding more of his followers than he is willing to risk himself. On further reflection, Jesus already has found a few people willing to risk a great deal on his behalf. The man with the colt ran risk. The people who prepared the seder ran equally grave risk. Roman authorities are continually on alert for resistance and revolt. Doubtless those daring people are sympathizers and threats to the state. It occurs to me that following Jesus might well include moments of great risk, yet I feel peculiarly alive when I hear Jesus' invitation and his challenges.

Blessings to you,

Eli

Biblical Reflections

🖜 Picture yourself walking with Jesus through Jerusalem. Imagine your walk during the day, in bright light. Fear and anxiety wilt in daylight. You may want to picture your walk with Jesus at dusk, when shadows deepen. The story about risk taking struck a nerve. The careful man ended up punished. You want to ask Jesus for clarification. Now you have an hour alone with Jesus when you can ask him to explain what he has in mind. What do you to ask? How do you pose the questions to him?

🖜 Clearly the story and Jesus' own life present risk taking as a dominant theme. Picture yourself sitting with Jesus in a candlelit room. The streets of Jerusalem have long since darkened. Fearing that someone might overhear, you speak in subdued tones. Jesus takes you seriously. You dare to confess your hesitance to take too much risk. He knows the stakes. He reveals to you that he is convinced he will not get out of Jerusalem alive. The chill night air and his comments cause you to shiver. Jesus needs you to pray for him. Offer a prayer for Jesus so that he will continue to have courage enough to follow God's will through to the end. What do you pray?

Contemporary Reflection

Imagine Jesus sitting in on a committee meeting at your local church. Someone suggests a project, and Jesus reacts to the proposal. Remember that Jesus has told stories about people taking risks. His own life authenticates risk taking of the highest order. What does Jesus say about the risk taking that he perceives in the committee's proposal?

Note your reactions as you followed the suggestions for reflection. Describe any comfort, discomfort, or new insights about yourself or about Jesus in your journal. What implications for your life might come from this encounter with scripture?

Day 30

🕊 READ LUKE 20:1-18.

My Good Friend,

Constraints of time and space prevent me from describing
all that has happened in Jerusalem up to this point.
However, from what I have written you must sense how
dramatically the tension between Jesus and religious
authorities has escalated. All of us feel increasing stress.
Quite honestly we wonder why Jesus chooses to create
more stress in Jerusalem of all places at this time of year.

Today Jesus sparred again with chief priests, scribes,
and elders. They wanted to know where Jesus received
authority to speak and act as he does. In typical fashion
Jesus turned the question on them. These men want to
take Jesus seriously, but they don't know how.
Controversies cluster around three issues: authority,
power, and control. These dynamics don't sound
particularly "religious." However, if you boil down the
discussions, the arguments, and the positions to their
essence, you find these three dynamics in play all the
time. How else do we make sense of the conflict between
Jesus and religious authorities? Jesus seems to have little
concern for their emphasis on minuscule points of
tradition and law. Clearly he threatens their authority. He
can take a question designed to trip him up and turn it to
make a point. I can imagine how frustrated the religious
authorities must be when he won't argue on their terms.

I have a further thought about the issue of power. Jesus makes real things happen over and over again. People have been healed: Some have had their sight restored; others were enabled to walk. I don't mean to disparage the work of priests and others who work in the Temple and synagogue. We always need priests to conduct worship, scholars to teach the scriptures, and managers of the organization. However, monitoring how people act or think does not do anyone much good. Jesus' power, by way of contrast, seems to release creativity and imagination. Jesus has certainly stirred my imagination. He has triggered thoughts and concerns that I never would have imagined before meeting him. I remain grateful for what he has allowed me to learn and how he has set my imagination loose. I respect the power and authority of anyone who sees the love of God in a father's care and of anyone who cares about individuals as Jesus does.

It doesn't surprise me at all that Jesus has upset some of the conventional thinkers, the "rules and regulations" people and traditionalists. They can't match his authority even by quoting ancient authority. They can't match his power with anything they say or do. People who are hurting will seek Jesus.

Anger against Jesus underscores our anxiety. Anger against Jesus has begun to harden into resolution. Some people intend to get rid of Jesus. This anger scares me. It surely must scare Jesus. I want to see how Jesus handles this situation. Will he be as good on his feet as he's been in the past? Will he equal the forces being mustered against him? Time will tell.

Dare I wish you peace? Yes, I will.

Eli

Biblical Reflections

🌱 Eli dreads the forces that gather against Jesus. He wonders whether Jesus can be equal to the hostilities that mount against him. Read Luke's narrative of Jesus' entry and initial conflicts in Jerusalem. Allow yourself to feel the escalating tension. How can you help Jesus?

🌱 Jesus tells a story of a man and his vineyard (20:9-18). To a careful listener Jesus seems to tell a story that portends his own death. Imagine yourself listening to the story for the first time. You want to erupt, "God forbid!" Now imagine yourself, for the first time, realizing that Jesus recognizes death as the conclusion to his work, preaching, and teaching. Up until this point you have been able to tolerate the increasing conflict. You have been able to sustain courage even as tension escalated. But now you feel the first shudder of fright. You know Jesus cannot forever escape the people who intend to get him. As much as you may have wanted to flee, you have fought that impulse. You've decided to remain with Jesus. However, you know that you don't have the spiritual resources that will carry you to the end. You can only pray an interim prayer, one that will sustain you until tomorrow. What do you pray?

Contemporary Reflection

You find yourself in an uncomfortable spot. Imagine yourself in the midst of a group meeting (a church, business, or civic group) where you have tried to explain your perspective on a particularly explosive social issue. At least one person in the group does not agree with your point of view. Angrily that person demands, "What makes you think that you're right?" Consider the tone of that accusatory question. Jesus may have heard just such a tone when Pharisees questioned him. Now imagine Jesus addressing the same issue that you have addressed. He too wants to speak to your group. He takes a position similar to yours. Again someone demands, "What makes you so certain?" How does Jesus respond? What does he say? What is Jesus' tone of voice as he answers? To what sources does Jesus point when he gives his answer? Imagine your surprise and near delight when Jesus says, "In all honesty, I agree with [*your name*]."

Note your reactions as you followed the suggestions for reflection. Describe any comfort, discomfort, or new insights about yourself or about Jesus in your journal. What implications for your life might come from this encounter with scripture?

Day 31

My Good Friend,

Thank you for your letter of last week. Yes, discipleship increasingly draws me to Jesus. I began this journey in Galilee. In those days, which seem a long time ago now, Jesus intrigued me. I told you that I felt comfortable looking at Jesus from a distance. However, since then I have seen Jesus close-up. Jesus' grasp of the human condition, his vision of what is possible, his insight into the purposes of God, and his own personal courage have been remarkable all along this journey. Nowhere has he been more insightful and courageous than he has been during these days in Jerusalem. He's really something under pressure.

All of us who have been following Jesus recognize the opposition to him, which builds every day. His enemies reveal their secret now. Of course Jesus does not defuse the explosiveness of the moment. His stories always have an edge to them, and even now he continues speaking in riddles and ambiguities. Let me give you an example.

Taxes create a constant source of conflict. In a thinly veiled attempt to catch Jesus off guard, a group of people challenged Jesus with the question *Should we pay taxes?* In an instant he sized up the group, the question, and the underlying intent of their question. Not that he would have answered much differently if a disciple had asked precisely the same question. Jesus said we should give to the state what the state demands and we must also give to God what God requires. You want to talk about people sputtering in their mug of wine. Jesus refused to give these questioners anything remotely seditious in his reply. "Give to Rome what is Rome's" can hardly be twisted to be treasonous. It means, "Pay your taxes." However, he went further, saying we should give to God what belongs to God. Now, what does that mean? As always, Jesus makes the listener responsible for that determination. Jesus' opponents have to grant him the former declaration and allow for the latter interpretation.

Jesus captured the dilemma in which we all must live. We must live within the limits of the empire. Only a complete anarchist would argue that we tear down all systems and institutions. And even an anarchist eventually would have to organize the anarchy! Nevertheless, we are not merely ciphers on the state's tax lists. We are people who have multiple loyalties. We will always have decisions to make about how to use our financial resources. I will say it bluntly. We shall always have to decide how much to give to the purposes of God.

If Jesus had given an unequivocal answer, he could have alleviated much anxiety. He simply could have told us how much to give and when. Instead his answer puts responsibility squarely in our hands. He may have avoided capture by his opponents but in doing so he put disciples in a rough spot. Disciples must decide how much and what belongs to God.

I told you that I feel myself to be more of a disciple. I feel a peculiar vibrancy when I am with Jesus. When he talks, my own thinking is quickened. When he tells stories, my imagination races. I don't know how to say it other than that I see differently, feel more deeply, and perceive more imaginatively around him. I can't claim much else except to say that he stirs something soul-deep.

Blessings to you,

Eli

Biblical Reflections

☙ Eli says he sees differently because of Jesus. What would happen if you were to look at a circumstance as Jesus might look at it? How would it appear? What prevents you from seeing as Jesus sees?

☙ Jesus refuses to get caught in an "either/or" question. He sees another set of possibilities. He refuses to allow the question to limit his thinking. For what question in your life do you find "either/or" inadequate and a "both/and" resolution desirable?

Contemporary Reflection

What would Jesus say to someone who declares, "America, love it or leave it"? What might Jesus have to say about any demand for unequivocal patriotism? Imagine talking with Jesus about the demands made on citizens of the United States. What are we to do when we sense conflict between what we believe to be legitimate claims of the government and legitimate claims of God?

Note your reactions as you followed the suggestions for reflection. Describe any comfort, discomfort, or new insights about yourself or about Jesus in your journal. What implications for your life might come from this encounter with scripture?

Day 32

☙ READ LUKE 21:5-36.

My Good Friend,

Tensions build in the city. The number of people grows to
fill the city to capacity, as every year at Passover. As usual
lots of people try to determine what all the signs of the
time mean. A number of people ask Jesus about when the
kingdom will come. I could have told them that they
waste their breath. Someone told me that Jesus doesn't
even know the time.

Rather than speculating about timing, Jesus launched
into a long description filled with lurid images and all
sorts of catastrophes. As he spoke, I could almost hear
the tumultuous sounds and smell the odors. Mind you, I
don't get caught up in that sort of thing normally. I have
quite enough on my mind without all that. However,
with hostility so thick that we can almost touch it, the
sights and sounds Jesus describes come more quickly into
our imaginations. As he spoke, one detail especially
caught my imagination.

In the midst of catastrophe people will have a chance
to bear witness to the truth of God's purposes. If I recall
correctly, Jesus said, "This will be a time for you to bear
testimony." There will be no warning, no time for
preparation. We will not have time to practice a speech for
the hour. Instead the demand will come unexpectedly.
What each person says will be authentic and spontaneous.

To tell you the truth, Jesus' words and descriptions frighten me. I prefer advance warning and time to get ready. I do not like questions for which I have not prepared an answer. Invariably when I am asked or put on the spot, I ask for a little more time to think and to formulate an educated opinion. From what Jesus said, I assume that all of us will be required to give our witness and that our witness will be what is already in us.

I do not mean to sound as if I can explain things of the end time any better than others can. Jesus places the burden of responsibility squarely on the disciple. When Jesus implies the urgency of the moment, he suggests that critical moment could come at any time. Any one of us could be "on the spot." As to how we prepare for that dramatic moment, I have no insight. As to how we prepare spiritually, Jesus gives no indication. Jesus is certain that we must stand and bear witness.

That's about as much sense as I can make of Jesus' teaching. From talking with others I gather that they are equally as concerned and uncertain as I am. We all agree with Jesus' assessment of history and the current climate. We will face catastrophic events in which people will be required to stand faithfully and be ready to take a moral stand. I hope it does not happen to me!

Faithfully,

Eli

Biblical Reflections

🕊 Eli feels frightened when Jesus speaks of catastrophic events that will engulf faithful people. Jesus describes the events and circumstances. What does his face look like as he speaks? Look at his eyes. How do his eyes show weariness from the wear and tear of the past few weeks? How can you tell that he is anxious about his own capacity to bear witness to God's truth?

🐦 Imagine talking with one of the disciples. He says, "I'd like to have that moment back so that I could say . . ." What moment does he want to retrieve? How could he have been better prepared?

Contemporary Reflection

You have a chance to sit with Jesus and talk about the events of September 11, 2001. You want to ask Jesus how he interprets those dramatic events. Imagine Jesus speaking about those events in a fashion similar to his depiction of events that would engulf Jerusalem. What do you want to know? Imagine Jesus offering to say a prayer. For whom does Jesus pray? What does Jesus say about enemies? How do you feel as Jesus insists that he means it when he says we should pray for our enemies?

Note your reactions as you followed the suggestions for reflection. Describe any comfort, discomfort, or new insights about yourself or about Jesus in your journal. What implications for your life might come from this encounter with scripture?

Day 33

❧ READ LUKE 22:1-13.

My Good Friend,

Tonight I write about events that terrify me. I feel
overwhelmed! We discovered to our horror that a
conspiracy to arrest Jesus exists. Officials are looking for
an opportune moment in which to seize Jesus. Rumors
have been circulating all week long. I have dreaded this
moment. Why does power that conspires against good
seem to work so effectively while goodness appears
terribly weak? I want desperately to help Jesus, but I can
do nothing. I heard about the plot too late. The rest of the
disciples and Jesus have gone to a private home for what
may be their last supper together. I thought about hiding
because I didn't want to get caught in the same snare set
for Jesus. But I changed my mind: I didn't want fear to
rule my life.

The brutal truth: If people in power decide they want
to get someone, they can. Officials always find people
ready and willing to carry out orders. Sooner or later
someone cracks. Someone forms the weakest link. I've
heard a rumor that Judas broke—that he has gone to the
officials and made arrangements to reveal Jesus' location.
We have all suspected that a small group of people want
to do away with Jesus.

I feel as if I am watching a race, a contest between the
forces of good and the forces of evil. The forces of evil

now have the lead. The forces that would do away with Jesus can employ every means possible to capture him. Jesus, on the other hand, works through subtle means and must await people to join him. Do you suppose Jesus has known that the conspirators were putting into motion forces to engulf him? If he knows and still proceeds with his plans for a supper, I have to admire him all the more for his courage.

I am sitting in my room and writing very quickly. I am sorry to be so brief, but something has to break soon. The strain has been unbearable. I don't know what will happen tonight. I hope the disciples and Jesus can somehow avoid the trap!

I told you that all of this overwhelms me,

Eli

Biblical Reflections

❧ Imagine yourself in the room where Judas meets with authorities. What conversation do you hear? Describe Judas's posture. How do you picture the officials? What reasons does Judas give for revealing the location where Jesus can be found? In what ways can you identify with Judas?

❧ Assume for a moment that you have learned of the plot to trap Jesus. Though you run grave risk by doing so, you want to warn him and the disciples. You want to help him avoid capture. During an hour before the disciples and Jesus gather for their supper, you are able to meet privately with Jesus. Jesus refuses to seek an escape. To your horror you realize that Jesus will not flee. You've heard too many stories about what happens to people when they fall into Roman hands. You have but a few moments during which to try to discern what Jesus thinks at this crucial moment. You want to ask Jesus how he has such courage. Ask him. How does he respond? With time running out, you have one more question. You want to ask Jesus to grant you more of the faith you need to live as courageously as Jesus lives. Jesus looks at you, extends his hands for the final time to you, holds your hands, and prays a brief prayer for you. He prays for faith equal to the need and courage for the hour. You want never to forget his final words to you. Write Jesus' prayer that he prayed for you. Then include a prayer for Jesus to have sufficient faith for his hour of need and courage for his moment of peril.

Contemporary Reflection

Most of us have experienced final moments with friends or family. We have known those moments when the finality of life and death emerge all too apparent and real. Imagine sitting with Jesus in a place near where you live. For the moment you remain alone and safe from prying eyes and listening ears. You may never have a chance to see him again. What do you want to say to Jesus? What do you want to thank him for? What in his ministry have you found most helpful?

Note your reactions as you followed the suggestions for reflection. Describe any comfort, discomfort, or new insights about yourself or about Jesus in your journal. What implications for your life might come from this encounter with scripture?

Day 34

READ LUKE 22:14-38.

My Good Friend,

You know how much I enjoy sitting down to a fine meal with good friends. The disciples attended what turned out to be a memorable occasion and their final meal with Jesus. I recalled other meals. You remember the old stories, don't you? Abraham greeted unnamed visitors and hosted them. Those same visitors announced Sarah's impending pregnancy. Elisha set a banquet table for a captured army and thus set into motion a cease-fire agreement. That memory haunts me to this day. Also, I think of the Israelites in their frantic efforts to get a few things together and a bit of baked bread to escape from Egypt. Who can forget those meals? Those are all from our tradition. I am also thinking of meals to which Jesus has been invited in the past.

Remember those suppers Jesus shared with Pharisees? Jesus obviously liked having a good time and a fine meal. Some critics pointed to his relishing a good time. Remember how they compared the Baptist's austere disciples to Jesus and his disciples who always enjoyed a sumptuous meal? I overheard one sourpuss accuse Jesus of gluttony. By the way, I never did go to worship with that fellow. Long-faced religion doesn't do much for me. Who can forget Zacchaeus? Who would have guessed that lunch at his house would result in that little man's refunding everything he had gouged from his neighbors? Any other rabbi with even a moderate amount of common sense would have known better than to be seen in his company, but it didn't bother Jesus at all. Jesus seemed to have the time of his life.

Suppers have a way of evoking memories, don't they? I have friends who always tell stories of meals they attended and places where they enjoyed fine food.

The final meal Jesus and his disciples ate together also held memorable moments. Passing some bread, Jesus said that the bread was his body, about to be broken. At the end of the meal he passed a goblet of wine to all of them and said, "Drink all of this." I don't think I shall ever forget that moment. As far as remembering, I suspect that as often as people who know Jesus sit down for a meal, someone will remember. This Passover meal in Jerusalem could be the last meal Jesus shares with his disciples. How he ever managed to keep his composure when all around him conspiracies are being hatched and his own disciples arguing with one another, I'll never know.

Pray to God that our memories are good ones filled with laughter. I hope as well that we will recall moments of high courage in the midst of trial and tribulation. Those will be fine meals.

Blessings to you,
Eli

Biblical Reflections

❧ Imagine gathering with the disciples for their final meal with Jesus. As you enter the room, you can smell the food: meat, bread, and fruit. Listen to the sound of wine splashing into each goblet. Smell the aromas filling the room. Where do you sit? Notice Jesus' posture. How does he handle the bread? You've seen him serve meals before. You've seen him break and distribute bread many times. Watch his hands, paying careful attention to how he handles the bread tonight. Listen as he says, "This is my body, which is given for you." What tone of voice does Jesus use tonight? Describe your feelings.

❧ As you sit with Jesus and his disciples around the table, each disciple relates a favorite moment from the months and years of following Jesus. Stories come from days in Galilee, the journey to Jerusalem, and in Jerusalem. Now you have been asked to tell your favorite story. Which story comes to your mind? Why did you choose this story as your favorite?

Contemporary Reflection

Imagine Jesus as a guest in your home for the evening meal. You ask Jesus to say grace. To your surprise, he says not only grace but all the words of the Communion ritual. Imagine Jesus taking one of the dinner rolls, breaking it, and saying, "This is my body . . ." Then imagine him, at the conclusion of the meal, taking a long-stemmed wine glass and saying, "This is my blood . . ." Jesus tells you that he never intended for the last meal to be enacted solely as a church ritual. He intended for every meal to be a remembrance. Enact the gestures and the words of the Lord's Supper during a meal in your home. Imagine Jesus as the guest of honor. Describe your feelings in Jesus' presence.

Note your reactions as you followed the suggestions for reflection. Describe any comfort, discomfort, or new insights about yourself or about Jesus in your journal. What implications for your life might come from this encounter with scripture?

Sixth Sunday in Lent

READ LUKE 13:31.

My Dear Friend,

I have mentioned Pharisees only sparingly over the course of my correspondence. I have attempted to understand what their concerns are and why Jesus has sparked so much controversy and conflict with them. If you listen to some people, you would think that conflict with the Pharisees constitutes the major focus of Jesus' entire ministry and preaching. I have always been concerned about understanding people as real individuals who have noble motives and authentic concerns. Let me explain.

I hesitate creating a false portrait easily dismissed by any meager argument. The Pharisees, with all their concern to jot and tittle, remain some of the most ardent adherents to Torah and tradition. As I have mentioned earlier, these emphases have been our salvation. I cannot argue with them at this point. In fact, a fair amount of what I hear today about a return to the basics, back to the Torah, all sounds good to me. Indeed it sounds like what the Pharisees advocated generations ago. You and I have talked about this. We agreed that the initial movement became a means by which our people survived.

However, we also agreed that the Pharisees' initially worthy initiative has hardened into a rules-and-regulations orientation. Among my concerns is this: We may be tempted to think that the problem of the Pharisees belongs

145

uniquely to them. They are real people, just as we are. An inclination to rigidity, what I call a "pharisaical impulse," resides deep in all people. Therefore, we cannot afford to point fingers accusingly. Remember how Jesus himself told us not to criticize others for what lurks in ourselves? For every demand the Pharisees make on people, the followers of Jesus may make a similar demand on their disciples. I suspect that in the future the movement that has begun to form around Jesus may develop a similar pattern of demanding strict adherence to tradition at the expense of caring for real people. A day may come when Jesus' followers form an institution as rigid as the Pharisees' system. I am not ready to criticize all Pharisees as if they are evil incarnate. They are not.

I hope that Jesus' followers will not lump all Pharisees and all Jews into one mass. A widely disparate people shouldn't be misinterpreted as a homogeneous group. Such an attitude risks dehumanizing the people in the group. Imagine condemning all Jews because Jesus is a Jew! Imagine treating all Jews poorly because of conflict between Jesus and some of his fellow Jews. Imagine treating Jews inhumanely in the name of Jesus, the Jew who taught us how to be fully human and humane.

Thus, I confess my concerns. To some these modest protests disqualify me from following Jesus. One person suggests I am not fit for the Jesus movement. That may be. I will run the risk of taking Jesus seriously. I continue to come to terms with his demands, and I try to see life from his perspective. I want people to feel as safe with me as they feel with Jesus.

Blessings to you,

Eli

Biblical Reflection

Read Luke 13:31, one of the most overlooked verses in Luke's Gospel. Not all Pharisees harbored animosity toward Jesus. Imagine sitting with Jesus when word from concerned Pharisees reaches Jesus. A good friend sits with you. Both of you always accepted the conventional wisdom that Jesus and Pharisees didn't get along. However, here Pharisees express genuine concern about Jesus' safety. He does not seem surprised that some Pharisees show concern for him. You have a chance to talk with Jesus. What do you want to ask him? How does he answer you? What does Jesus have to say to you when you reveal your prejudice against Pharisees?

Contemporary Reflection

You suspect that you have some "pharisaical impulse" within you. You have reviewed requests regarding changes in the worship style of your church. You tolerate some changes, but other changes simply are not comfortable. Moreover, you cannot picture worship without certain components. You want to check with Jesus to see what he has to say. In a moment that feels a little like confession you reveal to him some elements you consider essential for a good worship service. What does Jesus say?

Note your reactions as you followed the suggestions for reflection. Describe any comfort, discomfort, or new insights about yourself or about Jesus in your journal. What implications for your life might come from this encounter with scripture?

Day 35

My Dear Friend,

Everyone wants to be a hero or heroine. When the sun shines and no clouds cast shadows, everyone imagines performing heroically in the midst of terrifying events. But none of us know what we might do until we find ourselves in the midst of real pressure, real life-and-death decisions. One of Jesus' strongest disciples was shocked at his own reaction in such a situation.

Peter claimed that he would go to prison or even die for Jesus. Peter declared that, even if the other disciples would not, he would demonstrate that kind of courage. Jesus, with uncanny insight, gently said, "No, Peter, tonight you will have three moments when you will deny even knowing me." Jesus left it there with no further elaboration.

Events then tumbled over themselves. No words do justice to the terrors of that night. After supper we went across the valley into the darkness of an olive grove. In the middle of the night police shattered the silence. Within a matter of seconds, they arrested Jesus and whisked him off to the high priest's house. Few of us recall exactly what happened. After a big meal, some wine, in the near total darkness we could barely see anything, much less make sense of it. When the police crashed through the trees and shouted orders for arrest, fear paralyzed us.

They were after Jesus. When Jesus had been removed, we tried to settle our shattered nerves. Thankfully the police arrested no one else. They didn't want any of the rest of us. We all tried to shrink into the shadows, but for the moment it appeared we had eluded harm's way. At least most of us had avoided harm's way. For Peter his night of terror had just begun.

Jesus' terrible prediction about Peter came true. Three different times that beloved disciple denied even knowing Jesus' name. I cannot blame him. I have been scared before, and I know that talking about what you'll do in a crisis often does not match what you actually do in the heat of battle. I hesitate to recall the number of times I boasted about what I would do if challenges confronted me. Others failed, but I never thought I would. I did not even entertain the possibility of moral failure. I bragged that I would be equal to any challenge. That's not the case anymore. I'll tell you what I've not told anyone else. I have been scared and broken. Now, instead of bragging as a kind of whistling in a graveyard, I have compassion for Peter.

How incredibly tragic that the final conversation between Peter and Jesus consisted of a boast and a terrible prediction. Peter will take that memory to his grave. My fear grows with each passing day of this week. Standing at the edge of the crowd in Galilee cost a lot less than standing close to Jesus here in Jerusalem. What happened to Peter could easily have happened to me. I don't think we've seen the end of this.

I must close,

Eli

Biblical Reflections

🥀 Eli speaks of personal failure. Few can read about Peter's denials of Jesus without feeling twinges of anxiety. Imagine yourself in that courtyard. The soldiers arrest your friend and take him away. Initially you don't know what else they will do or where they will take him. While attempting to glimpse your friend, you hear a disquieting voice. "Didn't I see you with him?" someone asks. You fear that you will be considered guilty by association. How do you respond?

🥀 Assume for a moment that you have been standing with Peter. You note that Jesus catches Peter's gaze. What do Jesus' eyes look like? What details of the scene most impress you? You don't want to forget anything. The other disciples will ask for a report. What do you say to comfort Peter?

Contemporary Reflection

After these awful moments, Peter goes off by himself. Eli finds him and tries to help by saying, "Remember how Jesus spoke of forgiveness? Now it's time to count on that." Imagine Jesus standing with you today. Jesus asks you to tell him about a moment when you felt as if you had failed him, when you denied Jesus. Listen as Jesus assures you that you are forgiven. What do you want to say to Jesus? Listen to him speak again. He says, "You are forgiven." What response do you make? What resolve do you make?

Note your reactions as you followed the suggestions for reflection. Describe any comfort, discomfort, or new insights about yourself or about Jesus in your journal. What implications for your life might come from this encounter with scripture?

Day 36

❧ READ LUKE 22:63-71.

My Good Friend,

What kind of person gets pleasure from mocking another person? I heard what happened to Jesus: mocked, belittled, scoffed at, and bullied by another. Why? I confess that I feel both rage and utter sorrow.

Why do some people need to belittle or demean someone else in order to find contentment? Do they have such an insufficient sense of self-worth that they must make others less? These questions swirl in my thinking as I imagine what Jesus must have experienced.

My best explanation is that people act this way because they want to make their opponents less than human. Only if they see the other as less human than they can they treat them in inhuman ways. Which of us, for instance, could beat a person nearly senseless if we knew him by name? If an individual looks different from us, beating becomes easier. If we consider the enemy not fully human, we can treat those individuals with malice.

Jesus, from Galilee, reveals his difference with his up-country accent and manner. Small wonder, then, that men can rough him up. They don't know him. He appears to be different. Ironically this man who always asked for people's names becomes a "no-name."

Speaking of names, people have been trying for months to pin Jesus down regarding his true identity.

Many people have pressed him about whether or not "messiah" labels Jesus. No one has yet received a straight answer from him. He continues speaking in riddles. I heard that in the heat of the moment a soldier smashed him in the jaw. Jesus muttered through broken teeth and a split lip that, even if he did tell his captors that he is messiah, they would not believe him. When they demanded a clearer answer, or rather as they continued to beat answers out of him, he replied in yet another riddle, "You say that I am." Ways to get at the truth, other than resorting to a severe beating, elude officials. I now recall ways Jesus drew out the truth from people. He cared for them, asked them for their names, invited them to lunch, and invited himself to supper. He healed, preached, and taught. Almost before they knew what they were doing, people found themselves revealing information and concerns that they had tried to keep secret for years. Why can't other people take a cue from Jesus?

Sadly, I must close,

Eli

Biblical Reflections

🙠 In one of the most brutal moments in all of scripture, police beat Jesus. They then interrogate him. Imagine standing near enough to the chamber that you can hear the sounds of men beating Jesus. Listen to the grunts of men trying to hurt another man. When Jesus finally utters a few words, what does he say?

🙠 Jesus remains alone, surrounded by angry police intent on beating him either into submission or nearly to death so that he will confess as the government wishes. Standing with Peter at a distance, you manage to get close enough that you can hear the shouts from inside the room. What do you hear? Peter whispers sharply, "What can we do?" You must answer, "We can pray." You and Peter utter a prayer on behalf of Jesus. What do you pray?

🌿 Altruistic thoughts have long since left you. In the pitch black of midnight you stand by yourself, huddled in the darkest shadow, hoping to remain unseen by anyone. You care about Jesus, of course; but in your heart of hearts you care more about avoiding the torture Jesus endures. What do you do when there's nothing you can do?

Contemporary Reflection

Citizens of your country have been exposed to videos of people being beaten and shot. Some of these awful images come from war. Other scenes have been videotaped on city streets. As you saw these lurid images, you wanted to say or do something. Imagine the scene in which Jesus is beaten. Suppose someone had had a video camera at that time. "What do you hope to accomplish by taping that awful scene?" you might have asked. What does the person with the camera say? Sometimes one can only pray. You have seen videotapes of beatings and death. You have read a story of Jesus being beaten to within an inch of his life. Write your prayer for these situations.

Note your reactions as you followed the suggestions for reflection. Describe any comfort, discomfort, or new insights about yourself or about Jesus in your journal. What implications for your life might come from this encounter with scripture?

Day 37

READ LUKE 23:13-25.

My Dear Friend,

I wish I could write another kind of letter. However, I must report and reflect on the awful events that engulfed Jesus. As we all feared, the officials managed to manipulate the crowd.

Everyone I've talked with has seen all too much Roman brutality. Romans punish insurrection particularly harshly. I cannot imagine how anyone could design execution by crucifixion. Nor can I imagine hating anyone enough to inflict that kind of horrible torture. The Romans figured out a perverse way of avoiding responsibility for the execution. You will recall my contention in a previous letter that people humiliate and debase others in part because the worst can be done to another who is different. Today, with that exact dynamic in play, a terrible choice was made between Jesus and Barabbas. I stood in the crowd, trying to be as unobtrusive as possible.

This city knows Barabbas for all his boorishness. He killed a Roman soldier and went to jail. Jesus, for all of his reputation in the north, remains largely unknown in this city. Pilate offered a terrible choice to the crowd. One of the two men—Jesus or Barabbas—would be executed by crucifixion. That means people would watch one man suffer a horrendous death, while the other man would be released. I could have announced ahead of time what the choice would be. How could a mob know anything about an up-country preacher? So when it came to deciding which man they could tolerate watching die a horrible death, the crowd chose Jesus of Nazareth. The crowd chose Barabbas to be released. I wanted to protest. Then I felt someone standing close to me. He whispered, "If you speak against Barabbas, you will find yourself at the end of a sword soon enough." That scared me. As much as I wanted to protest the injustice of it all, I kept quiet for fear of my life.

Though Peter's name is associated with moral weakness and failure of nerve, I have to be honest with you. The time came when I could have said something but, because I was scared, I didn't say a word. I now pray for an insight that might redeem this awful moment. Perhaps moral failure forms a necessary part of learning that we really cannot rely on our own strength and ourselves. Can we ask for and expect some kind of extraordinary power when we have a hard moral decision to make? That seems almost too good to be true. I have a second thought. My decisions, even if a crowd appears to overwhelm them, can make a difference. My voice in the middle of that crowd might have made a difference. Oh, if I hadn't been so scared, I might have made a difference in the crowd's choice. But what if our choice and our voice make no difference whatsoever? What if I had protested, and that harsh-voiced man ordered my crucifixion too? What good would my protest have been? For that matter, I wonder if, in a city of this size and in the entire empire, the death of any one person makes any difference. If a voice makes little difference, what then of a death? And if no one notices my death, will they notice Jesus' death?

There, I've said the unmentionable. I hope you won't mind that I have entrusted this to you, my good friend. I trust neither crowds nor majority rule.

I continue praying for peace,

Eli

Biblical Reflections

✸ Imagine yourself standing next to Eli in that crowd of people. Listen to the governor's charge. You may select one man for release and the other for death. Yes, you may want to select Jesus. What do you know about Barabbas? How do you feel about the fact that Barabbas has done what many of your friends have wished that they could do? They too want hated Roman soldiers out of the city. Emotionally you are with Barabbas. What about Jesus? You have heard only snippets of information about him. Speaking on Jesus' behalf tempts you. A rough voice from behind you whispers angrily, warning you that any protest will be treated harshly. What do you say?

✸ At least part of the scandal of the gospel is that Jesus looks like any other man. Nothing about him on that balcony commended him for release. Allow yourself to feel the fear Eli felt when someone stood next to him and whispered the threat. What can you do?

Contemporary Reflection

Imagine yourself leaving the scenes of Jesus' arrest and interrogation and the scenes of Peter's denials. You wish that you could have done more. Now consider your life today. Is there any circumstance in which you wish you could have done more, in which you could have been stronger if not heroic? Describe it. Now imagine talking with Jesus. What do you want to tell him? "Jesus, I wish I could have _____, but I didn't."

Note your reactions as you followed the suggestions for reflection. Describe any comfort, discomfort, or new insights about yourself or about Jesus in your journal. What implications for your life might come from this encounter with scripture?

Day 38

⨂ READ LUKE 23:26-31.

My Dear Friend,

I have followed Jesus for a long time now. What began in
Galilee now concludes in Jerusalem. I don't know how
else to phrase it: All that Jesus attempted to do, to say, and
to be seems a terrific gamble. A substantial following
gathered around him. The crowds gathered around him in
Galilee inspired me. Watching people flock to his teaching
in synagogues inspired me too. In fact, I felt the inspiration
and joined, at least at a distance. Now, however, with
these horrible events in Jerusalem, I wonder about the
staying power of the movement.

    I've seen and heard too many people who just do not
grasp Jesus' message. I've seen many moments of great
insight that people disregard as inconsequential or
irrelevant. If people do not understand his teaching and
preaching, how many will understand his death? What
makes Jesus think that his death will be any more
memorable or lastingly embedded in our imaginations
than anything else he has said or done? What if only a
handful of people understands the significance of his life
and death? If people don't get the point of his stories, how
can Jesus expect people to understand his Story?

    Jesus' whole enterprise always invites debate. If people
cannot fully understand Jesus this side of the grave, then
how can anyone expect the movement to continue after

his death? I hesitate putting any of this into writing lest it be misunderstood, but it seems important to talk openly and candidly about the liabilities, the perils, and the sheer iffiness of all of his life, ministry, and now death. For my part, I find authentic questions and concerns more important than mere mouthing of assent. Since I have come this far, I might as well continue my thought. I suspect that those of us who ask frightening questions and dare to express doubts participate in the movement equally with those for whom questions and doubts seem never to occur.

The nature of Jesus' teaching invites people like me into the circle. I cannot remember a time when he taught, preached, or spoke without a constant chatter of debate. Do you suppose the day might come when people in the movement will insist on agreement and unanimity? How ironic, if in the name of the one who taught with riddles and ambiguity, followers insist on a distinct absence of ambiguities and questions.

I felt included in the movement because I was allowed to think, to bring my questions, to express my doubts and concerns. Jesus never turned away from me. Throughout his work Jesus consistently demanded rigorous thought. He expected people to talk openly with him. I recall his eyes dancing when he debated with the Pharisees. I recall Jesus more than once saying that simply keeping a tradition does not constitute faithfulness. Instead he insisted that we keep the chatter going, discuss, and act on the basis of the best we know. He wants us to work within the demands of real life and keep the goals of the kingdom in mind. I began at the edge of the crowd and felt as if I might move farther away. Now, however, I feel as if I have moved closer to the center, closer to Jesus.

I will continue to take Jesus seriously and to continue the conversation around his teaching, preaching, healing; indeed, his whole life. I realize that many will never get the point. But that's part of the risk that Jesus embraced.

Filled with hope, I remain,

Eli

Biblical Reflections

❧ Eli contends that the ministry and life of Jesus equal an enormous gamble. What if people do not understand him? What if his riddles remain riddles? What if his miracles do not point to anything beyond a wonder-worker? Allow yourself a moment's imagination. Instead of Jesus as the immediately recognizable man in the center of a crowd, picture Jesus as an obscure, easily overlooked man. What does he look like? How does his talk command a hearing? How does he work with people so that others notice?

❧ Ambiguity feels either inviting or off-putting. How does ambiguity feel to you? Are you more comfortable regarding Jesus' parables as having many possible interpretations or as having only one interpretation? Why?

Contemporary Reflection

Eli reveals that he has moved closer to Jesus. Standing at the edge of the crowd no longer satisfies. Imagine that you have a chance to talk with Eli about your faith and relationship with Jesus. Picture yourself with Eli going for a walk around the area where you live. During the walk, Eli recalls other similar moments when he and the disciples walked with Jesus. Eli tells some stories and speaks of how he has grown closer to Jesus.

When he stops talking, it's your turn. He asks you to tell him some stories about how you have seen Jesus. He asks you for your favorite stories of Jesus. Which stories will you tell him? Which stories are your favorites? Tell him a story or two that illustrate the time that you too stood at the edge of the crowd. Then tell him a story that illustrates how you moved from the edge of the crowd to be closer to Jesus.

Note your reactions as you followed the suggestions for reflection. Describe any comfort, discomfort, or new insights about yourself or about Jesus in your journal. What implications for your life might come from this encounter with scripture?

Day 39

๛ READ LUKE 23:32-49.

My Dear Friend,

Writing this letter breaks my heart. Though I wanted to stand almost anywhere other than on that hillside, I decided to stay as close as I could. Today they executed Jesus of Nazareth. Three men had been led to the awful, ghastly place.

Not surprisingly one of the other condemned men cursed the soldiers, the crowd, God, anyone. The other man remained remarkably silent. He suffered his agony and torment stoically. Jesus had a different way about him. Grunting soldiers hammered spikes, bones shattered, men screamed, women shrieked, flies buzzed, and the air stank with the stench of death. In the midst of all this horror, I heard Jesus gasp a few words.

I weep as I mention his first words. I've told you time and again how many times Jesus had met people and uttered those most welcome of all words, words of forgiveness. They all flashed through my mind as I heard him say, "Forgive them. . . ."

What he said next came as a bit more of a surprise. Jesus glanced at the silent man. "Today you will be with me in paradise," he whispered. I thought to myself, what a dubious honor to dwell with Jesus in paradise, especially if the price for transport to that place is crucifixion! Yet, Jesus offered a promise of a better place, a better life.

The final words I barely heard. Jesus had reached his last breath. Understanding this dying person's last words competed with my unbearable sorrow. Nevertheless, those of us who talked about it later agreed on what we heard. Jesus said something about committing his soul to God.

I tremble brokenhearted now and cannot write much more. I cannot explain anything more about the events of this day or the words Jesus muttered. I will tell you this: The way Jesus died today speaks profoundly to me. Some people die with only a blank sky to hear their cries. Jesus died speaking to God. I remember someone's asking me, "How would you like to be remembered?" At the time I didn't know how to answer. After today, I think I know what I'd say. I would like to be known for how I died. If I should have any power of my faculties in those final hours, I hope that I would die with something like faith on my lips. I would rather be known as someone who trusted God rather than one who cursed an empty sky. If I should ever talk with Jesus, I want to talk with him about this. I wish to die as a man who has faith, confidence, and commitment to God and God's purposes. I'd like to be known as a man who lived to the highest calling. It's a long way from the faith that I didn't have at the beginning to the faith that I feel emerging. It's a long way from Galilee to Jerusalem. I remain glad that I walked with Jesus.

Blessings to you,

Eli

Biblical Reflections

🐟 Eli wants to flee from that terrible place of execution. He also wants to be near Jesus. Which of the two emotions stirs within you? You want to remain near Jesus but can barely tolerate watching a man die. Occasionally you look away in an effort to distance yourself from that awful scene. Yet you still return. Listen to the sounds of that dreadful place. Listen to men gasping for breath. Listen to the sounds of flies buzzing around dried blood. You find yourself wanting to say a prayer, but you don't know what to pray. What do you pray? How do you pray for Jesus during these awful hours?

🐟 Jesus utters three statements. How does his voice sound at this late time? Which of the three statements resonates most with you?

🐟 Listen to the people standing around you. To which word do people react most strongly? Some people continue scoffing at Jesus. Which of Jesus' final utterances seems lost on the people near you?

Contemporary Reflection

Imagine Jesus standing in the center of any of the trouble spots mentioned in the news today. Picture him trying to talk with the people on opposing sides. They exhibit anger, frustration, and little patience. They tell Jesus awful stories. They speak of endless violence, suffering, and death. At length Jesus speaks. He says simply, "Enough. Now is the time to forgive one another." The simplicity of his message touches you. You realize that revenge will lead only to more violence, suffering, and death. Briefly you wonder how Jesus can say something this simple. Then you realize Jesus uttered a word of forgiveness as he died and long before anyone asked for forgiveness. Imagine Jesus speaking today.

Listen to him ask God to forgive all that has been done. Talk with Jesus about the hope of forgiveness. You want to believe in forgiveness, but you don't know how. Ask Jesus to increase your faith. What do you say to him? What does Jesus say to you?

Note your reactions as you followed the suggestions for reflection. Describe any comfort, discomfort, or new insights about yourself or about Jesus in your journal. What implications for your life might come from this encounter with scripture?

Day 40

🌱 READ LUKE 23:50-56.

My Dear Friend,

Over the course of these months I have written a lot of words. You graciously received them. You read them carefully and wrote back to me sensitively. Today I ask your indulgence. Please understand my silence today. Jesus of Nazareth died yesterday.

I think my heart will break. Life was different around Jesus. I loved the way he used to tell stories. He had that marvelous sense of timing and that wonderful twinkle in his eye. I'll not soon forget how it felt to walk with him along the coast of the Sea of Galilee. To think of never walking those paths again causes great pain. And when I think that I shall never again have a chance to hear his voice, oh, how that upsets me. He had such a way with words, inflections, and tone. I can never forget how he said my name. I can also hear him say other names. The way he called the Gerasene man by name changed my thinking. Referring to people by adjectives never bothered me until I recognized that Jesus would not allow that. He asked for names, always names.

I always felt more fully alive when I accompanied Jesus. I saw things I had never seen before. He pointed out the red and white poppies growing wild on the hillsides of Galilee. I can still see him standing knee-deep in the water, enjoying the sunrise at Capernaum. He watched people closely. I won't soon forget how he smiled and pointed out the foibles of people. But he never left it there. He drew a lesson from behavior. I should also add that he never belittled anyone. Jesus was always consummately gracious when it came to working with real people in real circumstances. I always felt safe in his company.

I don't know how else to say it. I have never felt more fully alive, had my senses more quickened, my imagination stirred, or my thinking so thoroughly challenged by anyone. I shall miss him. Oh, how I wish he had not died.

I must close as I cannot write another word.

I wish you well, friend,

Eli

Biblical Reflections

🌱 Eli suffers the loss of a good friend. If you have stood next to a grave, you know how Eli feels. Keep in mind that Christians read the Gospel of Luke from a post-Resurrection perspective. Eli must suffer through the longest day in Christian memory: Saturday. Picture Eli as he remembers what has happened over the past few months and years. He saw great hope in Jesus. Now it appears to be ended. The man to whom he had been drawn, the friend in whom he had found life, and the one person in whom he had seen hope for everyone is now dead and buried. Sit with Eli. How might you console Eli? How does Eli respond to your consolation?

🌱 Allow yourself to sit with a friend under a tree. You have walked with Jesus and listened to him speak both publicly and privately. But Jesus is gone now, and you have only memories. Take a few minutes to recall the moments that linger with you. Remember how you felt, what you heard, what you saw. Now tell your friend about your favorite moment. What will you say to your friend about a man who stirred unfamiliar feelings and did unfamiliar things?

Note your reactions as you followed the suggestions for reflection. Describe any comfort, discomfort, or new insights about yourself or about Jesus in your journal. What implications for your life might come from this encounter with scripture?

Easter Sunday

READ LUKE 24:1-35.

My Dear Friend,

Today's letter differs from anything I've written in the past. I have just returned from what has to be the most exciting conversation I've ever had. Last night I couldn't sleep at all. Early this morning I went to eat breakfast with a few of the disciples.

I learned that when the women went to the tomb before dawn, they found the grave empty. Their report is more than most can believe. But they insist that they speak the truth.

The grave does not hold Jesus' body! As I've told you, Jesus said a lot I did not understand, at least not at first. Now I hear that his body is not in the grave. How can this happen? Words fail me. The sheer joy of it overwhelms me. The hope of it stirs me more deeply than anything I could have imagined. Jesus is not dead! There, I've said it. I can hardly believe the words that I have heard from my own mouth. Jesus lives.

Jesus lives; all that he promised is still possible. All that he did can still be done. All the hope he stirred remains a lively hope! The possibilities extend endlessly.

Since I have had only a few minutes to consider this and I am still someplace between grief-stricken and delighted, one major possibility occurs to me. Since Jesus has died yet somehow still lives, forgiveness does stand a chance. Clearly a few people have done their best to silence Jesus. They have attempted to make a lie of everything he said and did. Had they been able to execute him and keep him forever in a grave, then they might have succeeded in their attempt to silence him. But he lies not in the grave. Therefore, all that Jesus stood for remains possible. My good friend, I will tell you this: I pray that forgiveness does stand a chance because I see it as the hope of the world.

I should conclude with another personal word. I began following Jesus almost on a lark. For quite a while I kept distant from him. However, the more I saw and heard, the more he appealed to me. I felt a peculiar awakening of my soul. I know that may sound strange coming from me. Nevertheless, as time passed I felt drawn increasingly closer to Jesus. I now think of myself no longer at the edge of the crowd. No, I am not one of the named disciples. No, I cannot explain everything. I won't even try. I will tell you I have found life as I never thought I'd find it. I have insights that I never would have received without Jesus' influence. I have sensed hope beyond anything that I had thought possible. As difficult as discipleship can be at times, I wouldn't go back to the edge of the crowd. I will stay as close to Jesus as I can. I shall hold fast to the hope of Jesus and resurrection. The purposes of God cannot be contained, not even by death.

I wish you well, good friend. The grace of God and the power of Jesus be with you.

Eli

Biblical Reflection

Because modern readers know the rest of the story, our imagination is often limited. We know how the story ends . . . or, perhaps more accurately, how the Story continues. We have heard of the Resurrection. We have listened to the stories of the appearances. We have hundreds, indeed thousands of years of Christian history through which the miracle of life after death has been repeated and interpreted. What happened to Jesus' followers on Saturday? How did they feel? What anguish stirred in their souls when they set out on a long walk? What did they expect to see? to hear? to feel?

We know how they felt. They felt as we do after we leave the cemetery following a casket's committal to the ground. After we've said the Lord's Prayer and heard the minister's benediction, we must leave. The flowers will wilt and the day come to an end. On the morrow there will be an empty place at the table, a phone number to remove from the directory, an address to which letters and cards will no longer be sent. We know exactly how the disciples felt on that Sunday morning.

Small wonder that the disciples, in Luke's narrative, barely notice the third person who joins them on the road to Emmaus. The text is clear. The travelers did not recognize the man who joined them. Incredulous that anyone could be ignorant of what only a few hours earlier had torn their hearts and ripped at their souls, they blurted, "Are you the only one who doesn't know what happened?"

Then, as with any death, the men rehearsed what had happened. This rehearsal is a part of the grieving that we all do. Listen to anyone talk about the final days and hours of a family member's or a friend's life. Inevitably the story of the last hours will be told. After the disciples finished their story, the unknown traveler began to work through the scriptures—in all probability the Prophets—indicating how the life and death of Jesus might be interpreted differently. Still the men did not comprehend.

Only when the unknown traveler joined them for a meal—during which he took bread, said grace, and broke the bread—did they recognize who was with them. They recognized Jesus in the breaking of the bread. Then they remembered that walking scripture study. Then they began to comprehend all that they had been a part of for those months and years. Only then could they begin to comprehend the miracle of Jesus' being present with them even after he had died and had been buried.

We might begin to appreciate the miracle of that first day by imagining a family member whom we have committed to the earth two days ago appearing among us during an evening meal.

Long before the resurrection became a doctrine—something to prove through illustrative stories—the resurrection was a miracle that exceeded all the miracles the disciples had seen. God had managed to bring life out of a tomb. Somehow, mystery of mysteries, Jesus of Nazareth, the man who had touched, spoken, healed, and ministered, was not confined to the limits of life as we see it. Nor was he restricted to the finalities of death as we know it. Rather, mystery of mysteries, Jesus lives and abides with us.

As we have encountered Jesus through the Gospel of Luke and through the imagination of a letter writer, so we can encounter and be encountered by Jesus. Pray God that Jesus encounters us.

Contemporary Reflection

Undoubtedly you have had a moment when you have said to yourself, *This must be what it was like when Jesus sat with his friends.* It may have been during a supper or during a holy moment of worship. Somehow you sensed that the depth of relationship, the intimacy of the moment, the unspoken communication, and the emotions that swelled within you must surely be a hint of what the kingdom of God might be like. You wanted to continue the moment, to keep the feeling alive.

Recall that moment; now imagine Jesus sitting with you during that moment. He too senses that "all is well" with your soul. Now the two men who walked the road to Emmaus join you. Jesus sits with you unrecognized. But there is something special about how he refers to the prophets and the stories in the Hebrew Scriptures. There is something special about how he looks into people's eyes. As he reaches for the bread, says a word of thanks, and breaks the bread to pass it around . . . you recognize him. You have seen him in your midst.

The miracle of the Resurrection is not restricted to an event to which a handful of people were given insight on the first day of the first week following Jesus' trial and execution. Rather, the miracle of Resurrection is when we recognize and know the presence of Jesus who is alive and present with us.

P.S. to those reading this cache of letters

My prayer is that through the Gospel of Luke, these letters, and through imagination, we have been able to sit with Jesus at a table, along a roadside, on a park bench, in a coffee shop, in an ancient place, or perhaps even in our hometown. Whenever Jesus has been present with us, even in our familiar hometown, things are not the same, and we are not the same. The disciples were never the same again; nor will we remain as we were. The risen Jesus walks and lives with us.

Blessings,
Jim

About the Author

JAMES E. SARGENT is a writer, consultant, and teacher. He graduated from Defiance College and received his Master of Divinity and Doctor of Ministry degrees from United Theological Seminary. He served pastorates in the West Ohio Conference of The United Methodist Church. He has completed a Boston Marathon, plays guitar, and enjoys reading, walking, and writing.